The Giving of Grace:

The Nature of Salvation in Scripture

Doug West

Other books by the author
Pilot Light Christianity- The Danger of a Lukewarm Witness (Dust Jacket books)

"This is the generation of those who seek Him" –**Psalm 24:6a (NASB)**

P246 Marketing Group
P246.net

The Giving of Grace: The Nature of Salvation in Scripture
by Doug West
All rights reserved.

ISBN 978-0615829128

P246 Marketing Group
PO Box 984 Notre Dame, IN 46556

Cover design and all illustrations, Doug West
Book design, James Lovaas

Recommendations

"Sometimes when Christians talk about doctrinal distinctives, they get distracted. Rather than focusing on Jesus and all He's done for us and on God's Word and what it says to us, we wind up defending doctrines based on someone's perspective and try to win an argument. No matter who "wins" those kinds of arguments, usually lost people lose because we get distracted from our main mission—to make disciples.

How we see Jesus and what He's done for us matters…it makes a huge difference how we live both in the here and now and our view of the hereafter. Pastor Doug West takes an approach we don't see often enough…he looks at the issue of a believer's security by first asking us to stop and worship Jesus, look thoroughly at what God's Word has to say, presenting both main perspectives on the issue and then inviting us to make our decision. His focus is Jesus, not doctrine! If every believer made living for Jesus wholeheartedly their main focus, books like this would not be even necessary.

Thanks, Doug for being Jesus-focused, Word-based and gracious in "The Giving of Grace". No matter what your perspective about this issue, you always bring us back to Jesus."

Dr. Tim Roehl, Director of Training and Development
One Mission Society

"Insightful, instructive and simplistic in style. A unique treatise on the word grace by a pastor who has led many to faith in Christ. Grab a cup of java and sit back and enjoy Doug West's newest book."

Stan Toler, Bestselling Author & Speaker
Oklahoma City, Oklahoma

"An issue of great importance is the theological divide we call Calvinism and Wesleyan/Arminian theology. The real issue comes down to our understanding of how a sovereign God can love the whole world (John 3:16) and yet predestine some of those same loved ones to hell? In the Wesleyan camp we hold that free moral agency does not diminish God's sovereignty at all. My friend Doug West has written a handbook on this topic that shows both views and lets the reader decide what the Bible really says."

Terry Chapman, Pastor
Lighthouse Church of the Nazarene – Moravia, IA

Dedication...

To my loving wife, Priscilla, who encourages me in my projects, and loves me unconditionally. I am truly blessed to have such a loving wife and capable mother of my children. Two thumbs up!

To my kiddos (Matthew, Hannah, Dustin and Jayda) who are gifts from God. May you love Jesus wholly, and grow closer to Him with each year.

To Dad and Mom, for faithfully promoting and preserving the truth of God's Word.

To Nancy Swanson (my long time editor), whom I forgot to thank in my first book published, *Pilot Light Christianity*. Thanks for your witness for Christ and challenge to make me think grammatically and for making my writing look gooder (Ha!).

To the Pastors who helped:
Rev. Scott Melhoff- encouragement & suggestions early on.
Dr. Tim Roehl- encouragement, advice & editing.
Rev. Richard Reynolds- (The Prairie Lakes District's Apostle Paul) advice & encouragement.
Rev. Terry Chapman- insight, editing, and so much more.
Rev. Kirk Thorson- conversing & editing.
Rev. John Fetterhoff- friendship & insight from the Baptist side.
Dr. Stan Toler- encouragement to write & example.

To Gail Hanson,
Again to say that your (and Paul's) influence on my life has been profound would be an understatement. Thank you for your insight then & now on the subject matter of this book.

To James (Chris) Lovaas,
a long-time friend and encouragement, & now partner in ministry. Go P246! Rock on!

Last, but not least, to my Lord and Savior Jesus Christ, who gives meaning to this writing and fills out the great salvation being discussed. Thank you for Your Grace that reached me before I was ready for You (Rom. 5:8).

To all who will read this book who are honestly interested in the rules and boundaries of salvation set in Jesus Christ by God.

Table of Contents

Scripture Table

Genesis 20:6	John 10:11-15
Genesis 50:20	John 10:25-26
Exodus 34:24	John 10:27-29
Deuteronomy 4:29	John 12:32
1 Samuel 2:6-9	John 12:39-40
1 Samuel 2:25	John 15:16
1 Samuel 3:14	John 17:1-6
1 Kings 15:3	John 17:3
1 Chronicles 21	John 17:9
2 Chronicles 12:14	Acts 1:25
Psalm 75:7	Acts 11:21-23
Psalm 106:8	Acts 13:48
Psalm 106:46	Acts 16:14
Psalm 115:3	Acts 18:10
Psalm 135:6	Acts 18:27
Proverbs 16:4	Acts 26:19
Proverbs 19:21	Romans 3:10-18
Isaiah 10:5-13	Romans 8:5-9
Isaiah 25:1	Romans 8:15
Isaiah 45:22	Romans 8:28-36
Isaiah 53:11	Romans 8:38-39
Jeremiah 1:5	Romans 9:5-6
Jeremiah 10:23	Romans 9:10-13
Jeremiah 13:23	Romans 9:14-15
Daniel 4:34-35	Romans 9:16-18
Jonah 2:9	Romans 9:19-21
Malachi 3:7	Romans 9:22-23
Matthew 1:21	Romans 11:2
Matthew 7:18-20	Romans 11:28-32
Matthew 10:24-26, 28, 31-32	Romans 15:15
Matthew 11:27	1 Corinthians 1:30-31
Matthew 20:28	1 Corinthians 2:14
Matthew 22:14	1 Corinthians 3:16-17
Matthew 25:14-30	1 Corinthians 5:5
Mark 13:13	1 Corinthians 9:27
Mark 13:22	2 Corinthians 5:21
Luke 19:10	2 Corinthians 6:1
John 1:12-13	Galatians 1:15-16
John 6:37	Galatians 5:19-21
John 6:44	Ephesians 1:3-5
John 8:31-34	Ephesians 1:12-14
John 8:42-47	Ephesians 1:13

Ephesians 2:1-2
Ephesians 2:7-9
Ephesians 5:5-7
Philippians 1:27
Philippians 1:29
Philippians 2:22
Philippians 3:18
Colossians 1:21-23
Colossians 2:13
1 Thessalonians 5:9
2 Thessalonians 2:13
1 Timothy 1:15
2 Timothy 1:9
2 Timothy 1:12
2 Timothy 2:12
2 Timothy 2:25
Titus 3:5-7
Hebrews 3:6, 14
Hebrews 6:4-6
Hebrews 7:25
Hebrews 9:11-12
Hebrews 10:10, 14

Hebrews 10:26-29
Hebrews 10:38
Hebrews 12:1, 2
James 5:19-20
1 Peter 1:1
1 Peter 1:3-5
1 Peter 1:5
1 Peter 1:22-25
2 Peter 2:1
2 Peter 2:14, 18-22
1 John 1:5-6
1 John 2:19
1 John 2:25
1 John 2:29
1 John 3:9
1 John 3:10
1 John 4:7
1 John 4:19
1 John 5:1
1 John 5:12-13
Revelation 3:5
Revelation 5:9

Foreword
"Here we go…"

Wow, what a potential powder keg, discussing eternal security. It's like walking a flare through a firecracker warehouse, a Viking fan wearing their jersey at Lambeau field; a gun control advocate at an NRA convention. If there is one thing that people seem to want to argue over in and out of the church it is eternal security: can believers in Christ lose their way eternally? This work started out as a book contrasting the five points of Calvinism with the five points of Arminianism. I had just finished up *Pilot Light Christianity*, when a discussion I had with a lady sparked the idea and need for *The Giving of Grace*. I mentioned where I was pastoring and she mentioned that she had actually attended under the previous pastor, but quit as she did not believe that you had to ask forgiveness every time you sin. She also was currently attending no church. I quickly said that the Bible says that "if we sin we have an advocate with the Father- Jesus" (1 John 2:1). She quickly back peddled and said, "Well, I believe that you can't lose your salvation." But you know what? She was right both times. The Calvinist/ Once Saved Always Saved position when examined at a microscopic level says both things: believers do not lose salvation…ever, and once sins are forgive, since it is a "once for all" deal, repentance after you are saved only restores fellowship, but does not restore salvation. We in the Arminian camp believe that salvation is not to be a "check your pulse" to see if you are still alive/ fearful experience on one hand, but neither is it to be a license to sin without impunity. If you exist somewhere in the middle between the two extremes, you find holiness. My brother-in-law, Mike, once explained his approach to discipleship. He points people towards God. This takes care of questioning if you are or are not saved, and certainly takes care of trying to live in sin and reside under the banner of "Christian."

This book finally took the shape of a manual for street level use in the parameters of salvation debate. A seasoned believer or pastor could certainly go to commentaries and theological books to answer their questions-by all means! But instead of having to cart around an armful of books and your Bible, what if the wisdom of the scholars was cached into a volume, with apologetical defenses for the Arminian position, as well as a brief understanding of what Calvinism is saying. The Giving of Grace defines what God has done with salvation- given it to us freely, though we do not deserve it. This manual can be used when sitting down with a person who has honest questions about salvation's ins and outs, or a quick guide when you are going to talk to someone, or have just talked to someone and want to "check the record." It is not to be a tool to beat up Calvinists with. That does not benefit the Kingdom. But my goal is to equip the church and answer honest questions.

I have tried to consult with many different minds to get a good picture of what this work should be. Many works have been written on eternal security, by persons smarter and more equipped to cover this topic. *So why this writing then*? God put it on my heart, so there must be a reason for one more book on the topic. A right understanding of salvation is so critical, because if the hope is false, then the salvation is "straw salvation." A wise mentor of mine once said, "Don't do what has already been done." So my desire is to bring the *cookies close*, making this confusing, deep, theology as simple as possible. I certainly do not want to just rehash what has already been said, but use the wisdom of the past to promote the doctrine of full Biblical salvation and holy living for today.

Questions about salvation have been in my life since I was a teenager attending Valley Christian High School, when a Bible class split into sides over losing salvation. A few years later when I lived in Milwaukee, Wisconsin and worked at a Pizza restaurant in whose owner upon learning my position on eternal security (Arminian) said, "Before you go home tonight I will have convinced you that your position is wrong!" Well, I was a fireball back then and accepted the challenge with eyes ablaze with holy might and determination. We proceeded to verbally duel over the two positions (Arminianism vs. Calvinism), throwing out Scriptures like Wild West gunslingers right and left, with the delivery drivers keeping track and finally asking, "So who is winning?" About that point in the debate all of my air went out and I began to ask myself, "What kind of example are we giving them?" Most of them were unsaved. Not a good example.

Looking back it reminds me of the scene in the movie "Big," when Tom Hanks plays the role of, Josh Baskin, a kid who grows up overnight into adulthood due to a fortune from a carnival ride. In one scene, the full size Hanks is playing hand ball against colleague Paul (John Heard), who is threatened by the youthful Hanks. They come to a disagreement in the game, and begin to chase each other, acting like two kids in a schoolyard brawl, in which they ran in circles around the yard, got in head-locks, and bloodied skin. Very close to the heated debate in Milwaukee. It was this debate amongst others that proved fruitless and just spun the conversation in endless circles. I don't want to be fruitless as a follower of Christ; I want to be about fruit. Another time in Sioux City, Iowa, while checking out at a lawnmower repair shop, the owner decided to argue theology as well. I must have commented on some tracts he had on the counter before long he shot off on "once saved always saved" and began to mechanically churn out Scriptures right and left. He was good at rattling off Scripture to fit his position in a timely fashion. I interjected Scriptures here and there, but he just droned on seeking to correct me. As I realized that this was like yelling in a fan, I looked for an out and found it when the phone rang and our business was over, so I left, making a timely getaway.

One misnomer I want to correct is that the Arminian position is a "you can lose your salvation" stance. A better understanding of the position is that security is found in the life of a "Believer". We in the Arminian camp believe that we are going to be in Heaven, secure as the Calvinists. I attended Liberty Baptist Theological Seminary online and had one peer once write on a message board, "Preach like an Arminian, sleep like a Calvinist." Well the point I believe Scripture makes is that believers <u>are</u> secure. Believers make up the elect (those filling out the numbers of those being saved). If someone has doubts they are not fully in the love of God (1 John 4:18). The real scrutinizing begins with the question, "what then constitutes a Believer?" Is a Believer a title conferred irreversibly, or is being a Believer descriptive of one who has taken hold of saving faith with accompanying works proving it (Jam. 2:17, 26). Is a Believer someone pre-picked (elect) by God decreed for salvation, or is a Believer someone who was given freewill by God, and activates membership in the community of the elect? Can a Believer ever cease believing? If so are they still a believer? Does this make them out of fellowship, or out of salvation? When does salvation begin? When does it end? Lots of questions to be considered when interpreting Scripture that are answered throughout this work in the appropriate comments on the Scriptures. I believe that Scripture titles and defines the "elect." One cannot be *titled* or *entitled* without having the works that define a living faith (Jam. 2:20).

The sovereignty of God has also been in the center of this discussion. My eyes have been opened to this quality of the Most High in a new light. The Arminian position emphasizes the freeness of humans within the hand of God. We believe in God's sovereignty, but it is within the realm of an All-Powerful God who lovingly has sought out humans with free-salvation. Now while He is a God that does not single out some and block others, He is All-Powerful and answerable to none. This powerful God does move and shape us without our knowing or consent. I have been in the right place at the right time numerous times in my life that could have only been brought about by a Sovereign God. From going to Vennard College while it was still open and Ralph Sprunk was teaching, to getting to work in outgoing mail at the Billy Graham Evangelistic Association in Minneapolis and meeting Billy the year we worked there, and on and on. Even in the last few months and days, I have seen the hand of God move in ways that I am reminded that I am clay and He is the Potter (Isa. 64:8). The point I am trying to get to here is that sometimes we try in the Arminian camp to down play the strong sovereignty of God, and end up stripping Him of too much of His sovereignty. God IS Almighty. God knows all, sees all, is all. He just isn't so strong to push past His love and subdivide salvation into the "have's" and "have not's" without a choice in the matter.

May this work challenge, equip, and guide you into a deeper walk with Jesus, who is the same yesterday, today, and tomorrow (Heb. 13:8).

–Doug West 2013

NOTE: This writing is to be a concise handbook for practical interaction with proponents of the "Once Saved Always Saved," Election/ Predestination position. For more in depth study I would recommend the following books (that are listed in the bibliography section): I. Howard Marshall, *Kept by the Power of God* (One of the best Biblically based studies of election and perseverance, written by a top-rate scholar, who is not from Wesleyan-Arminian circles); Robert Shank, *Life in the Son* & *Elect in the Son,* (Shank being from the Baptist camp and knowing the doctrines in and out, and finding them troubling).

"What's 'dis lose your salvation stuff?"

Introduction

    I remember early on not knowing that putting on the CAPS lock on the computer keyboard and WRITING EVERYTHING IN CAPITALS was a sign that you were YELLING at the person you were writing to. Somebody graciously explained this to me, after I had sent the whole e-mail to them in caps. They were like "Do you realized that writing in all capitals symbolizes yelling in an e-mail?" I was totally blown away, and embarrassed at my ignorance and action. Now I was wrong and didn't have the foggiest clue that I was wrong, until someone shared the right information with me. That is the point of *The Giving of Grace*, to get the right information into the hands of the right people. How will that happen exactly? Well, I believe that the Lord wants this information "out there" so He is going to link up people with this book so His purpose can be accomplished.

    That leads me to the purpose of this book. I firmly believe that everyone who is interested in the nature of salvation in Scripture in relation to God's grace needs to read this book and consider the information presented. As mentioned in the foreword, I have had enough encounters with the Once Saved Always Saved camp to be concerned enough about confused and doctrinally belligerent believers. The main reason for writing this book is because I believe the vast majority of the Christian world is operating off of some form of Calvinism, and often times this leads to flawed beliefs and flawed living. Is everything that John Calvin proposed flawed or wrong? No. If you read through His *Institutes* or *Commentaries*, there are lots of good things in there, but there is also flawed doctrine. So it is my desire to get the right information into as many hands as possible. Why? Because if there is flawed doctrine persisting, it can lead to flawed living and even into a false sense of security. What could be worse than believing there was security and finding that your equation was off just enough to miss out?

If you do not know much about the two doctrinal positions covered in this book (Arminian/ Calvinist) you will learn much about them in this book. This book is not the "end all, be all" on this debate, but it does have a good amount of information packaged as user friendly as possible. Some of the quotes may seem dated and wordy, but they help give credibility to the thoughts-showing the lengthy history of this discussion. If you will seriously sit down with your Bible and go over the texts in this book and look at a sample of both positions I believe that you will begin to see the big picture- that God loves everyone! And Scripture operates through that lens– love. If God is perfect love, then His relating to humans will mirror that perfect love, not hinder it.

Those holding to the Calvinist position may or may not heed to all that John Calvin proposed. Most will hold to (perseverance) or eternal security, while they may or may not believe not every one is called equally (election), or that God's grace is resistible (irresistible grace). One Professor at Liberty University was an Amyraldian (stresses universal atonement (particular application), and is a mix of Arminianism and Calvinism). So it needs to be understood that not all Calvinists or "once saved always saved" believers are carbon copies, but most likely hold to parts and pieces of what John Calvin taught. Most hold to eternal security or "once saved always saved," but may reach the conclusions of who and how they are saved differently.

This book is written to be read by people of either theological camp or beyond. If you are Armenian or lean that way, read this book! If you are Calvinist, or lean that way, read the book as well! I once had a seminary professor that said that he was confident in Christianity to the point that he would put it up against any religion out there, because it could stand its own. I feel the same way about the Wesleyan-Arminian position: it stands its ground. I am Wesleyan, because I believe that Scripture calls us to live holy lives above carnal living. I am Arminian, because I believe that the believer is secure "in Christ", the condition being "in Christ." That God has reached out to all of humanity impartially. That His grace touches all (believers can get deeper in God because they give more access). If you disagree…then you're wrong. Just kidding! If you disagree, write notes. Challenge yourself to be closer to God. A pastor friend of mine once said, "May we live above our theology." That is my prayer as well. May all of us live higher in Christ than we expect, and if we get something wrong, may He help us to right it and grow closer in fellowship with Him.

Church History
(This section on church history was largely influenced by Howard F. Vos'
book, *Exploring Church History.* I have tried to follow his outline of church
history as pertinent to the purpose of my book, and rewrite it. Other
sources have been used as well and will be noted.)

I will only give a brief summary of the Old Testament, as we will focus on
the history of the Church, but without the Old Testament there is no New
Testament or Church. God, who has revealed Himself as Father, Son, and
Holy Spirit has always existed and created the world with the purpose of
bringing His Great salvation to the human race. Knowing that mankind
would fail with the capacity of freedom (Genesis 3), His plan entailed
revealing Himself through the Law given to Moses that would set up a
system of worship that the Messiah (Jesus, the Son of God) could connect
to and give new meaning. God's people lived in cycles of falling away,
being oppressed, and repenting. God raised up key figures along the way
(leaders, Kings, prophets, etc.) to point people in the right direction. The
Old Testament sacrificial system was temporary and served to ultimately
point the way to Jesus (the perfect Sacrifice), was given ultimate meaning
and purpose in Christ.

Jesus Christ- Jesus the Son of God/ Son of Man, came to Earth to die on
the cross for the sins of humanity, according to the eternal will of God.
During Jesus' short ministry of 3 years, He invested in his 12 disciples
prepping them to teach His principles about the Salvation and Kingdom of
God. They would only accomplish this through the filling of the Holy
Spirit (Acts 2).

- **(C.E. 30-100) Early Church-** The book of Acts, written by Luke,
  shows the emergence and flow of the early church from Jerusalem
  "to the ends of the earth." James, Peter, and Paul would step up to
  be used to spread Christianity globally. The church was then
  comprised of those who gathered to not neglect worshipping of
  Jesus Christ (Heb. 10:25), and spreading His message of salvation.
  Persecution of the early church by the Jewish leaders was constant.
  By the end of the first century churches existed in cities the apostle
  Paul had visited in his three missionary journeys.

- **Constantine-** Persecution had dogged Jesus throughout His
  earthly ministry (Pharisees and Sadducees- Jewish religious leaders).
  This persecution continued to the early church by the Jews, as this
  new religious sect that followed Christ was gaining popularity and
  threatening their positions of leadership. As Roman persecution

fanned, the Church was tried and tested with many falling away, and others shining true unto death. Along came the Roman Emperor Constantine that, upon a vision of the Christian Cross, made Christianity the official religion of the empire (C.E. 311). His mother was also to have been a devout Christian and no doubt brought influence his way. Constantine's conversion was both good and bad. Good because persecution officially ended, but also bad, as syncretism (a merging of multiple religions) crept into the church. With this new partnership, various occult religions were merged with Christianity. Some dealt with this turn towards corruption by trying to remain true despite the decadence, others turned to monasticism and secluded themselves to be separate from worldliness.

- **Council of Nicea** (C.E. 325)- Denounced Arianism (that Jesus was born into existence/ not eternal). Declared Jesus begotten of the Father, same substance.
- **4ᵗʰ Century- The Canon of Scripture-** Formulated and endorsed by church leaders and at various councils.
- **Augustine (C.E. 386)-** Defended teaching that Adam's sin was passed by nature (original sin), promoted election and predestination, and wrote The City of God (his response to Christian's blamed for the fall of Rome). Predestination.
- **Schism in the Church East/ West (C.E. 1054)**

The Church began to flow towards one of two loyalty points: Constantinople, the Eastern Church, or Rome, the Western Church. Various differences set the stage for a parting of ways.

East	West
Icons (pictures) in worship	Statues in worship
Saw the Holy Spirit as proceeding from God the Father exclusively.	Saw the Holy Spirit as proceeding from the Father and Son.
Willing to be under Emperor.	Willing to nudge and guide the Emperor.
Both unwilling to submit to the other.	
Boundaries of each unclear.	
Cultural differences.	
Leavened or Unleavened bread in worship?	
Clergy to be clean-shaven?	
Clergy to be married or single?	

This is by no means an exhaustive list of study, just a snapshot of this point in Church History. At any rate the Church split in C.E. 1054, East and West.

- **Crusades (C.E. 1095)** - The attempt of European rulers to "retake" the Holy Lands for God, though economic, adventure, and other self-satisfying reasons crept in.

- **Inquisition (C.E. 12ᵗʰ Century) -** A move by the Roman church to deal with heretics in house, as opposed to by the state government, and keep the *flock* in line.

- **Scholasticism (C.E. 9ᵗʰ – 12ᵗʰ Centuries)-** A harmonizing of philosophy and theology, in which the teachings of Roman Catholicism were shaped and brought together, such as the sacraments and defining salvation, and God's existence.

- **Mysticism (C.E. 12 Century Concentration) -** An individualistic approach to salvation in response to the formal institutional church. It differed from Eastern mysticism as it separated creature from Creator.

- **Monasticism (C.E. 13ᵗʰ Century Concentration) -** Centers of learning, missions, and social welfare. Monasteries allowed some freedom in finding God, which sustained evangelical thinking in the Roman church until the Reformation.

The Reformation-
Leading Up To The Reformation...
Peter Waldo (C.E. 1140)- a wealthy merchant that got rid of much of his wealth to serve God. A Biblical reformer that believed that people should obey God rather than men (Roman church). Scripture was the sole authority as well.

John Wycliffe (C.E. 1330)- Bible translator, authority of Scripture, believed that Clergy were to help and serve, not rule.

John Hus (C.E. 1371)- believed that Christ was the Head of the church, not the Pope. Addressed the abuses of the church (Simony, Indulgences, etc.)

Savonarola (C.E. 1452)- was against worldliness and corruption in the church. Believed in Justification by Faith and the authority of Scripture.

Brethren of the Common Life (C.E. 14th Century)- tried to bring about a return to practical religion.

The Changing World...(C.E. 16th Century)

- **POLITICS**
  The rise of nation states began to challenge the power of the papacy (Roman Church).

- **INTELLECTUAL**
  -Humanism: a movement to enhance the experience of life and culture that brought about an interest in Biblical languages and the Bible.
  -Individualism: led Martin Luther to consider the priesthood of the believer, and not just the appointed priests, which called for direct access to God and His Scriptures.

- **RELIGION**
  -Decay: Religion in the middle ages became all about money and manipulation. Church offices were sold to the highest bidder (Simony), salvation could be purchased, and the clergy were more worldly than not.
  -Call for Reform: many movements and literature pushed for reform from with the church, paving the way for the coming Reformation.

- **SOCIETY/ ECONOMY**
  -Decline of Feudalism
  -Rise of towns/city states

- **Martin Luther- (C.E.1483)**
  -Lawyer (at father's urging)
  -Crisis (fell off horse due to lightning in bad storm)
  -Monastic life (in search of inner peace)
  -Study/ Teach
  -Concerned over the Indulgences in Church & works based salvation
  -Justification by Faith (came to believe this between C.E. 1513-1518)
  -(C.E. 1517) Concerned over indulgences (payment for a piece of paper that removed sins, for the living or deceased, per Roman Catholic Church). His 95 Theses, was a response to the system of indulgences that was affecting his parish, Wittenberg, though not sold there.

Luther's beliefs-
-Salvation by Grace alone
-Bible as authority (not traditions of men as in Catholic Church)
-Priesthood of Believer (all were called to share Gospel with others, not only clergy)
-Congregational Singing (as opposed to just the priest)

Break from Rome/ Protestantism (protest) begins

Calvinism becomes the dominant protestant belief system.

TWO MEN

To have a realistic picture of the issue of Calvinism vs. Arminianism we have to look at the two men that formulated each belief system. It is worth noting that not all that bears the name of "Calvinism," or "Arminianism" follows the original intent of John Calvin or James Arminius. Since this is not a lengthy biography, but a simple assessment of both theologies matched with Biblical principles, both men will be briefly compared in the following chart.

Name	James (Jacobus) Arminius
Date	1560-1609 (49)
Nationality	Dutch
Profession	Pastor, Professor
Theology in a nutshell	Resisted the formulating Calvinist Tradition; Freedom in God
Location	Leiden, Holland (died)

Name	John Calvin
Date	1509-1564 (54)
Nationality	French
Profession	Lawyer, Pastor during Reformation
Theology in a nutshell	Followed Augustinian Tradition: Strong Sovereignty of God, Predestination
Location	Geneva, Switzerland

Arminius

Followers formulated Five Articles of Remonstrance in 1610
1) Total Depravity
2) Conditional Election
3) Unlimited Atonement
4) Prevenient Grace
5) Conditional Preservation

Calvin

RESPONSE: Synod of Dort (1618) (TULIP)
1) Total Depravity
2) Unconditional Election
3) Limited Atonement
4) Irresistible Grace
5) Perseverance of the Saints

John Wesley
Dates: 1703-1791
Wesley would be in agreement with Arminius on the five articles.
He would add in: Entire Sanctification (to deal with neutralizing depravity).
Those adhering to this track of thought would be considered: Wesleyan/ Arminian
Not all Arminians would be considered Wesleyan as some are (Baptist, Reformed, Charismatic, etc.)
Wesley's Order of Salvation: Original Sin, Prevenient Grace, Justification, Sanctification, Glorification

Understanding the Two Sides: Arminianism & Calvinism
So what are these beliefs exactly? In this section we will break down the Five
Points on both sides to give a clear picture where each camp is coming from.

<u>Arminianism</u>

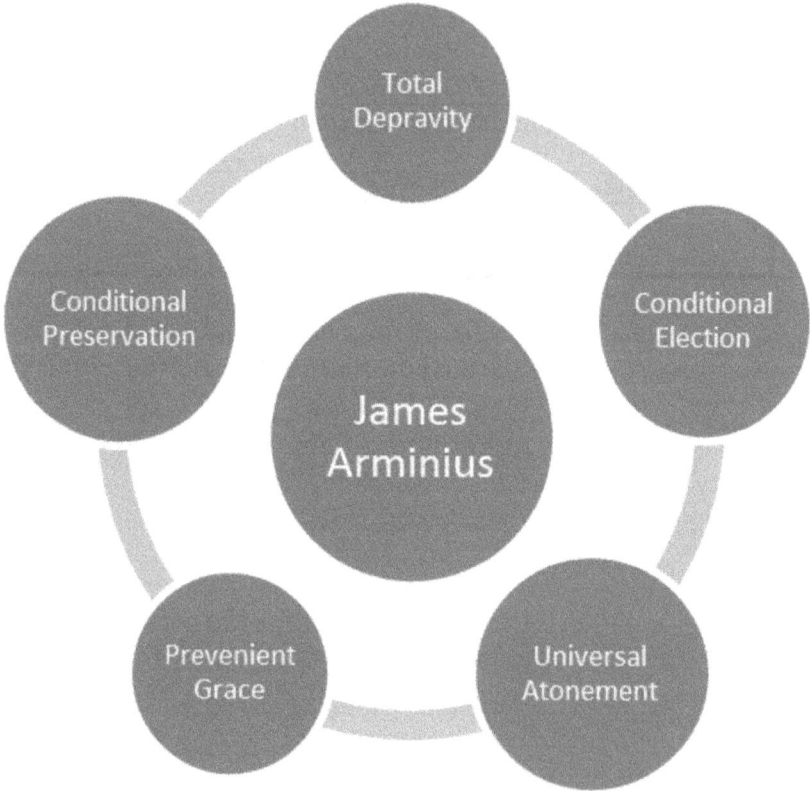

Total Depravity- Fallen spiritual nature from Adam (Original Sin). God
provides grace to enable spiritual restoration through sanctification.
Conditional Election- Faith in Christ enables one to believe and be elect.
Universal Atonement- Christ died for the whole human race, though not all
will be saved.
Prevenient Grace- God's, grace that goes before, draws the sinner, activates
salvation and sanctification by faith. This grace is not mere human
determination, but God granted and instigated grace.
Conditional Preservation- the Believer is secure as they actively remain "in
Christ." God's grace never stops calling the sinner on the run, but freewill
allows for a departure from grace.

Many Variations but similar strain…

Overall idea is God grants freedom to interact with Him in salvation history, while accomplishing His purpose. IT IS NOT an exercise of the will of humans apart from the grace of God (as some have falsely assumed).

Groups holding this view: Oddly some Baptist groups, some Evangelical Free, The Evangelical Church (of North America), Conservative Methodists (Free, etc.), The Church of the Nazarene, The Salvation Army, Wesleyan Church.

Calvinism

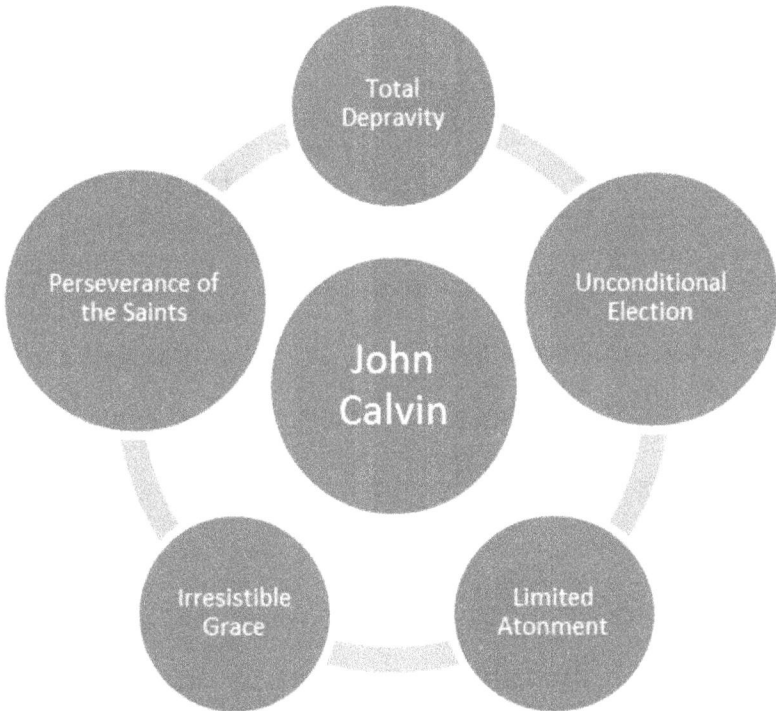

Total Depravity- Due to Adam's fall humans are irreparably fallen and must sin in thought, word, and deed. God has already saved the human, before they believe.

Unconditional Election- Due to God's decree before time began, those He has called will be saved since they have been chosen from eternity, those not called will be lost as they never had a chance.

Limited Atonement- Christ died for the elect, not those who will be lost.

Irresistible Grace- Those who are truly saved cannot become unsaved, as they were pre-planned by God to be saved and must be saved.

Perseverance of the Saints- The saved will remain saved (not dependent on faith) because God has decreed it. Faith follows the decree of God; believers believe and have faith as a result.

Many variations but similar strain…

Overall idea is that God has determined a fixed structure of salvation history, Sovereignly divided into the eternally elect and eternally lost.

Groups holding this view:
Reformed, Presbyterian, Baptist, etc.

Arminianism-

Glorification- Taking hold of salvation in heaven and being integrated with perfections not available on Earth, but bagan there.

Sanctification- Started at salvation and fully developed for humans at entire sanctification. The sin nature is taken care of and out of the picture, being cleansed. The new nature and person are alive. Carnality is dethroned and dealt with in a lessoned state, more external as the internal is God's. The sin nature can regain ground and may need to be again shut down and the new nature brought back in by the Spirit.

Salvation- Eternal Life that is based on faith, with grace reaching out ahead. God has decreed salvation to be made available to all humans, though not all will believe.

Grace- The mercy of God that is ever a step ahead of humans, reaching out to sinner and saint. God's tool of freewill enables humans to resist His grace if so desired (but it is not an easy task).

Fall- The exercise of freewill by representatives of the human race that resulted in separation from God spiritually (and wholey). God's grace can restore the damage that was done spiritually through sanctification, though the human body will remain fallen.

GLORIFICATION
SANCTIFICATION
SALVATION
GRACE
FALL

Calvinism-
Glorification- Taking hold of salvation in heaven and being sanctified (carnality is gone).

Sanctification- Being set apart to God and experiencing the ongoing work of the Holy Spirit, but deparavity still remains for mortals.
Salvation- Eternal life that has been decreed for the elect. A person is saved before they accept Christ, as it has already been decreed and is merely activated.

Grace- The merciful gifting of the saints and kindness to deposed sinners.

Fall- The decreed sinning by humans that led to depravity. This fallen state cannot be fixed spiritually this side of heaven. The Spirit can speak louder than depravity, but will not alter or remove it, other than cover it.

Calvinism

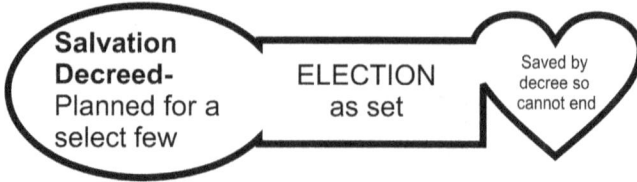

Arminianism

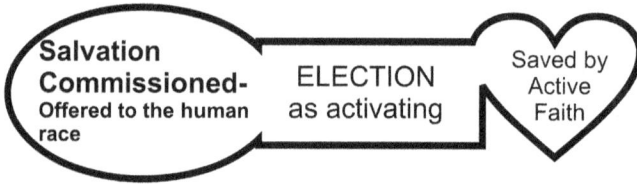

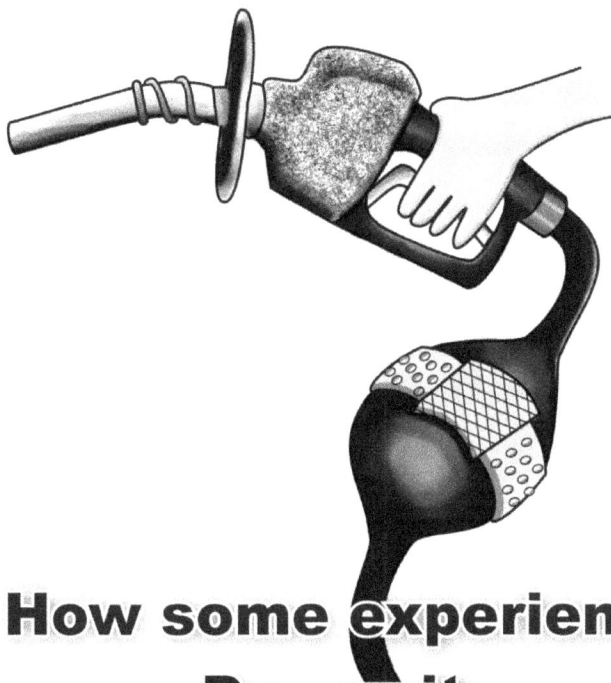

How some experience Depravity

Understanding the format used in the following study

Text: Bible verse or passage
Context: A snapshot of what the verse or passage pertains to in the Bible.

Calvinist View: Thoughts that would reflect Calvinism/ Once Saved Always Saved position. Thoughts not with quotation marks are my creation, based on interaction and study of Calvinism. The quotes are marked with authors names.

Arminian Response: Thoughts reflecting the Arminian and or Wesleyan position. Thoughts are mine, unless noted.

Comment: A short summary of what is going on in the passage and how it relates to our study, through an Arminian lens.

Quick Points: Short thoughts that summarize what you need to know about this passage.

From the Experts:

Wesleyan and or Arminian experts who have commented.

The Bottom line: A sentence or two summing things up.

The Note file pic is a place for any notes you want to add (other than those scribbled in the margins).

Notes:

Rightly Understanding Commonly Used (Calvinist/ Once Saved Always Saved) Proof Texts...

Old Testament

Genesis 20:6 (NIV)

[6] Then God said to him in the dream, "Yes, I know you did this with a clear conscience, and so I have kept you from sinning against me. That is why I did not let you touch her.

Context: Abraham deceives Abimelech

Calvinist View: This text shows God as sovereign, operating in election.

Arminian Response: This text shows God's sovereign prevenient grace at work.

Comment: God had kept Abimelech away from Sarah, Abraham's wife, due to His faithful and Sovereign nature. God takes care of those who follow Him. This is not God manipulating chess pawns, but the actions of a loving parent looking out for a misdirected child (Abraham), who is actively following Him. God can do whatever He wishes, but He does not step over freewill (which He has imparted to the human race).

Quick Points:

1) God sovereignly looks out for His own.

2) This is a case of the Almighty graciously having mercy on a godly man, not enforcing a love-less decree (that Abraham had no choice but to be righteous).

From the Experts:

It is God that restrains men from doing the ill they would do; it is not from him that there is sin, but it is from him that there is not more sin, either by his influence on men's minds checking their inclination to sin, or by his providence taking away the opportunity. It is a great mercy to be hindered from committing sin, which God must have the glory of whoever is the instrument. –John Wesley, *Explanatory Notes on the NT*

The Bottom line: God moves in the lives of people according to the big picture of who they will be in or out of Him.

```
Notes:
```

Genesis 50:20 (NIV)
[20] You intended to harm me, but God intended it for good to accomplish what is now being done, the saving of many lives.

Context: Joseph's reassurance of no revenge towards brothers, after Jacob (their father) dies.

Calvinist View: God's strong election at work– God willed Joseph to end up in Egypt.

Arminian Response: Election of purpose within the boundaries of freewill- God took Joseph to Egypt and used a free agent.

Comment: God used Joseph to be the agent of salvation for his family and the people of Egypt. He used a person whom He knew would draw near to and follow the ways of God. Joseph filled out godliness, as a godly person living out what was natural to him.

Quick Points:

1) God used Joseph's circumstances to bless many.

2) God took someone who would be open to godliness and shaped them. Joseph's freewill led Him God's way and God knew this would be the case.

From the Experts:

. - "He (Joseph) spake comfortably unto them, as in Genesis 45:8, telling them that he attributed the whole business to the particular providence of God." –Adam Clarke, *A Commentary and Critical Notes*

The Bottom line: God uses free agents to accomplish His purpose.

> **Notes:**

Exodus 34:24 (NIV)

[24] I will drive out nations before you and enlarge your territory, and no one will covet your land when you go up three times each year to appear before the LORD your God.

Context: Rebellion of Israel, Covenant broken/ Renewed

Calvinist View: Sovereign election– God's promise to drive out the non-elect.

Arminian Response: Salvation history being set up through freewill– God judging sin and opening the path for a foundation for salvation.

Comment: God sovereignly chose the Israelites to enter the Promised Land and to be the holy people the Messiah, Jesus Christ, would come to the world through. To do this required providential (preplanned) efforts to sustain the race that had been given the Promise of blessing and salvation through the Messiah. God acted out His plan fashioning persons in place and out of the way, according to how they would respond to His Divine grace.

Quick Points:

1) God moves His Divine plan through free agents who either choose Him and are blessed, or reject Him and are cursed.

2) It is through a perfect blend of Sovereign rule and human (God given) freedom that carries it out.

From the Experts:

- "They who have God for their protector have a sure refuge." –Adam Clarke, *A Commentary and Critical Notes.*

The Bottom line: God protects His own, and His own desire Him through freedom of choice.

Notes:

Deuteronomy 4:29 (NIV)
[29] But if from there you seek the LORD your God, you will find him if you look for him with all your heart and with all your soul.

Context: Moses' Message on Obedience

Calvinist View: This is God being faithful to His election of persons.

Arminian Response: This is God's grace being shown to the repentant sinner.

Comment: This passage speaks of yearning in exile for God who would respond. This is a simple salvation formula, not determining. If you seek God you will find Him. He draws on all, and He knows who will respond. It is a plain fact that the faithful respond in faith. Not coercion or pre-labeling. Proper responses from people who God knows will want to be godly.

Quick Points:

1) God pointed out early on that there would be punishment if the Israelites fell away from obedience to God.

2) Punishment for sin brings about the right state of mind and heart.

3) God draws those receptive to Divine Grace, not those who are like marionette puppets, forced to respond based on coercion.

From the Experts:

"Whatever place we are in, we may from thence seek him. There is no part of the earth which has a gulf fixt between it and heaven." –John Wesley, *Explanatory Notes on the NT*

The Bottom line: Seekers always find God, who is ever beckoning to them to come His way. God does not decree or limit who seekers are, but outlines what they do.

Notes:

Deuteronomy 29:9 (NIV)
[9] Carefully follow the terms of this covenant, so that you may prosper in everything you do.

Context: Moses' 3rd and Final Speech: Introduction of (Palestinian) Covenant

Calvinist View: The worst-case scenario was loss of temporal rewards, not eternal for the elect. "The covenant He made with their fathers would stand forever, but their enjoyment of its promises depended on their obedience to the obligations. –Warren Wiersbe, *Bible Exposition Commentary (BE Series) - Old Testament - Pentateuch.*

Arminian Response: The covenant had conditional and unconditional elements to it.

Comment: If the Israelites did not obey the covenant God would punish them, but make a way for His promise to continue for salvation History. Those disobedient would lose out altogether.

Quick Points:

1) The terms for security by covenant were conditional.

2) The longevity of the covenant would surpass individual humans, who would be judged eternally based on their response to the Covenant.

From the Experts:

"Both former mercies, and fresh mercies, should be thought on by us as motives to obedience. The hearing ear, and seeing eye, and the understanding heart, are the gift of God. All that have them, have them from him. God gives not only food and raiment, but wealth and large possessions, to many to whom he does not give grace. Many enjoy the gifts, who have not hearts to perceive the Giver, nor the true design and use of the gifts. We are bound, in gratitude and interest, as well as in duty and faithfulness, to keep the words of the covenant." –Matthew Henry, *Matthew Henry Concise Bible Commentary*.

The Bottom line: Obedience to God's Covenant was essential to spiritual survival.

Notes:

Deuteronomy 29:20 (NIV)

[20] The LORD will never be willing to forgive him; his wrath and zeal will burn against that man. All the curses written in this book will fall upon him, and the LORD will blot out his name from under heaven.

Context: Moses' 3rd and Final Speech, Warnings against apostasy

Calvinist View: "*The Lord will not spare him.* Moses here teaches us that the obstinacy in which the wicked are willfully hardened, shuts against them the door of hope, so that they will find that God is not to be appeased." "Thus, by Isaiah, God swears that this was an inexpiable crime, that, when He called them to baldness and to mourning, the Israelites encouraged each other to gladness; and, whilst feasting luxuriously, said in ridicule, "Tomorrow we shall die." (Isaiah 22:12.) By the word, הבא, *ahab*, Moses altogether shuts out the grace of God. Meanwhile he contrasts God's fixed purpose, — that He will not be willing to pardon, — with the depraved pleasures of those who take too much delight in their sins." –John Calvin, *Calvin's Commentary on the Bible*

Arminian Response: v.18, their hearts had tuned from God. God was concerned with persistent rebellion; caused by personal sin, not Divine decree.

Comment: Though God would continue His Promise of salvation and blessing, He would destroy and punish sinners. This was judgment on sin, not enforcement of a decree that made people set under sin and damnation.

Quick Points:

1) The people were warned to not sin and break God's covenant with them.

2) Sinning would reap immediate judgment.

From the Experts:

"The sinner is described as one whose heart turns away from his God; there the mischief begins, in the evil heart of unbelief, which inclines men to depart from the living God to dead idols. Even to this sin men are now tempted, when drawn aside by their own lusts and fancies. Such men are roots that bear gall and wormwood. They are weeds which, if let alone, overspread the whole field." –Matthew Henry, *Matthew Henry Concise Bible Commentary*.

"A prediction of Israel's failure and God's judgment." –*The Wesley Bible*

The Bottom line: Unrepentant rebellion is not forgiven by God.

Notes:

Deuteronomy 29:29 (NIV)

[29] The secret things belong to the LORD our God, but the things revealed belong to us and to our children forever, that we may follow all the words of this law.

Context: Moses' 3rd and Final Speech: Punishments for breaking the Covenant

Calvinist View: "…there is a comparison here made between the doctrine openly set forth in the Law, and the hidden and incomprehensible counsel of God, concerning which it is not lawful to inquire." –John Calvin, *Calvin's Commentary on the Bible*

Arminian Response: God makes known His secrets according to His purpose and grace. These secrets do not include predestination of certain people.

Comment: While God does not share all with humans, what He does not share, does not impact humanity apart from the course of holy love.

Quick Points:

1) God reveals only what we need to know.

2) His salvation is not contrary to His revealed holy, loving character that is not partial.

From the Experts:

"To this he answers, that the ways and judgments of God, tho' never unjust, are often times hidden from us, unsearchable by our shallow capacities, and matter for our admiration, not our enquiry. But the things which are revealed by God and his word, are the proper object of our enquiries, that thereby we may know our duty, and be kept from such terrible calamities as these now mentioned." –John Wesley, *Explanatory Notes upon the New Testament.*

"We are forbidden curiously to inquire into the secret counsels of God, and to determine concerning them. But we are directed and encouraged, diligently to seek into that which God has made known." –Matthew Henry, *Matthew Henry Concise Bible Commentary.*

The Bottom line: God reveals only what we need to know, and of that, it is not partial or evil, such as in selective election.

Notes:

1 Samuel 2:6-9 (NIV)

[6] "The LORD brings death and makes alive; he brings down to the grave and raises up. [7] The LORD sends poverty and wealth; he humbles and he exalts. [8] He raises the poor from the dust and lifts the needy from the ash heap; he seats them with princes and has them inherit a throne of honor. "For the foundations of the earth are the LORD's; upon them he has set the world. [9] He will guard the feet of his saints, but the wicked will be silenced in darkness. "It is not by strength that one prevails;

Context: Hannah's prayer of Thanksgiving to the Lord

Calvinist View: These are the two sides of predestination that serve God's sovereign purpose.

Arminian Response: This is God as Almighty and Sovereign working according to the big picture that includes freewill.

Comment: Only Almighty God has the right to move and mold, and fashion His created beings. His way does not always seem to make sense, as we do not always see the "big picture." This passage showcases God as in control, but v.9 reminds us that he works along clearly defined lines with the saint/ the sinner. He does not sacrifice their freewill in the process (which He gave them).

Quick Points:

1) God alone can act beyond our questioning.

2) He doesn't act apart from His system of freewill He has ordained in humans.

From the Experts:

"God is the arbiter of life and death; he only can give life, and he only has a right to take it away." –Adam Clarke, *A Commentary and Critical Notes*

The Bottom line: God does as He sees fit, but also keeps freewill intact.

Notes:

1 Samuel 2:25 (NIV)

25 If a man sins against another man, God may mediate for him; but if a man sins against the LORD, who will intercede for him?" His sons, however, did not listen to their father's rebuke, for it was the LORD's will to put them to death.

Context: The wickedness of Eli's sons

Calvinist View: Eli's sons were destined for destruction being non-elect.

Arminian Response: Eli's sons were judged for their personal sin, which fit into God's will and purpose.

Comment: The point here is that it was God's will to punish them for sin—not to act out a decree of judgment before action. To uphold His holiness and Name, God had to deal with the sin of the sons of Eli. It was not punishment based on a decision to single them out for judgment before the fact, but due to their destruction of His Holy ordinances and religious culture. To set people under judgment to satisfy just a decree, would rob God of His holiness, mercy, and justice.

Quick Points:

1) Eli's sons were punished for personal sins, not elected for punishment.

2) Sin and hardness brought judgment.

From the Experts:

"The priests persisted in continuing in sin, so God determined to destroy them." –*The Dake Annotated Reference Bible*

"(1) that God hath no pleasure in the death of him that dieth, and that He willeth not the death of a sinner, but rather that he should be converted and live;

(2) that the sins and the punishments of sin are accomplishments of God's eternal purpose."

– Albert Barnes, *Barnes' Notes on the Whole Bible*

The Bottom line: The ever-rebelling soul ends up at judgment for personal evil desires. They cannot be saved, because they do not want to be.

> **Notes:**

1 Samuel 3:14 (NIV)

[14] Therefore, I swore to the house of Eli, 'The guilt of Eli's house will never be atoned for by sacrifice or offering.'"

Context: Judgment on Eli and his descendants

Calvinist View: This is a prime picture of decreed election at work– Eli and his sons were eternally set to be non-elect.

Arminian Response: No Old Testament sacrifice was prescribed for willful sinning. This is not an eternal pre-positioning against the House of Eli, but post-sin judgment on future generations.

Comment: "That is, the punishment threatened against Eli and his family, shall not be prevented by all their sacrifices, but shall infallibly be executed." – John Wesley, *Explanatory Notes upon the New Testament.* Not that they were pre-set to be destroyed, but their willful disdain for the path of godliness would end in destruction.

Quick Points:

1) OT sacrifices were for unintentional sins.

2) This would affect the line of the priesthood as well as a curse passed down.

From the Experts:

"The sins of Eli could not be purged by the appointed sacrifices of the Law."

– Albert Barnes, *Barnes' Notes on the Whole Bible*

The Bottom line: God knew that this "line" of sin would not be repentant and thus, not broken.

> **Notes:**

1 Kings 15:3 (NIV)

³ He committed all the sins his father had done before him; his heart was not fully devoted to the LORD his God, as the heart of David his forefather had been.

Context: Abijah as King of Judah

Calvinist View: David was fully devoted because he was elected to be.

Arminian Response: David was fully committed to God and did not tolerate sin. God knew David would respond to His grace and knew He could make him great.

Comment: David was fully devoted to God, because he was a God-seeker. It was second nature. God rewarded and blessed this obedient desire for Him. God did not make him do this, but made His godly effort succeed and be blessed with the line of the Messiah. God planned all along to use David, but David could have chosen otherwise by Divine freewill, but didn't.

Quick Points:

1) OT sacrifices were for unintentional sins.

2) David was repentant as opposed to Abijam, who was not fully devoted to God.

From the Experts:

"His heart was not perfect—He was an idolater, or did not support the worship of the true God. This appears to be the general meaning of the heart not being perfect with God. –Adam Clarke, *A Commentary and Critical Notes*.

"Abijam's heart was not perfect with the Lord his God; he wanted sincerity; he began well, but he fell off, and walked in all the sins of his father, following his bad example, though he had seen the bad consequences of it." Matthew Henry, *Matthew Henry Concise Bible Commentary*.

The Bottom line: David was defined by a fully devoted, God-seeking heart. God knew who He would be and that as an obedient heart, he would fulfill God's will and desires.

Notes:

1 Chronicles 21

Context: David's sin of a census for pride

Calvinist View: Since David was an elect follower of Yahweh, He could not sin a sin to separate him from God.

Arminian Response: Since David loved God and lived out his godliness, as his heart yielded to God, this sensitivity to grace kept him from un-confessed sins.

Comment: Some commentators (J. Vernon McGee, etc.) view David's sin of making Joab orchestrate a census was at a heart level worse than his sin with Bathsheba. They also see this as a sin, but not a "salvation losing" sin. The point of Scripture is that if David had not repented, the destruction would have continued and ultimately his salvation would have come into question.

Quick Points:

1) Satan played on David's pride to get him to be interested in taking a census for military readiness.

2) This sin that resulted in numerous deaths, unrepented of would have been unpardoned, and unforgiven resulting in eternal judgment.

From the Experts:

"He sinned surely, but, after all, he was a man after God's own heart, and this is never more clearly manifest than in these dark days when God dealt with him for his wrongdoing." – G. Campbell Morgan, *An Exposition of the Whole Bible*

The Bottom line: As a free agent David sinned, and showed his true colors by repenting of his sin.

> **Notes:**
>
>

2 Chronicles 12:14 (NIV)

[14] He did evil because he had not set his heart on seeking the LORD.

Context: The Apostasy of Rehoboam

Calvinist View: Rehoboam accomplished his decreed position as a non-elect player.

Arminian Response: Rehoboam did not make the right choices (freewill), and subsequently did not find God, who was waiting for him.

Comment: Rehoboam had pagan ancestry that appears to have influenced him (Ammonite). This does not excuse, but helps understand how he got waylaid. It also shows us that Rehoboam exercised freewill. He veered off course that because God sabotaged him per decree, but his selfish desires.

Quick Points:

1) Rehoboam had a sinful ancestry (mother, pagan Ammonite).

2) He chose to live for self instead of God.

3) He did this, not God setting him under this state,

From the Experts:

"**Did evil** - Or, settled not, although he humbled himself, for a season, yet he quickly relapsed into sin, because his heart was not right with God. –John Wesley, *Explanatory Notes upon the New Testament.*

"Rehoboam was never rightly fixed in his religion. He never quite cast off God; yet he engaged not his heart to seek the Lord. See what his fault was; he did not serve the Lord, because he did not seek the Lord. He did not pray, as Solomon, for wisdom and grace; he did not consult the word of God, did not seek to that as his oracle, nor follow its directions. He made nothing of his religion, because he did not set his heart to it, nor ever came up to a steady resolution in it. He did evil, because he never was determined for good." –Matthew henry, *Matthew Henry Concise Bible Commentary.*

The Bottom line: Not yielding totally to God, is not living at all.

Notes:

Psalm 75:7 (NLT)
[7] It is God alone who judges; he decides who will rise and who will fall.

Context: Being Thankful for God's Righteous Judgments

Calvinist View: "God puts down one and exalts another." –Merrill F. Unger, *Unger's Commentary on the Old Testament*

Arminian Response: God sovereignly judges according to how people respond to His commands.

Comment: Anyone can judge, but only God judges righteously and fairly all the time. He fairly blesses and curse people based on their actions.

Quick Points:

1) Only God judges rightly (righteously).

2) God sees the whole picture and judges accordingly.

3) Only Almighty God is worthy of this right.

The Bottom line: God judges everyone fairly at all times.

Notes:

Psalm 89:33 (NIV)

[33] but I will not take my love from him, nor will I ever betray my faithfulness.

Context: David's Covenant & Lost Blessings

Calvinist View:

"Though the faithful answer not in all points to their profession, yet God will not break his covenant with them." –Geneva Study Bible

"(v.30) This passage teaches us, that when God adopts men into his family, they do not forthwith completely lay aside the flesh with its corruptions, as is held by some enthusiasts, who dream, that as soon as we are grafted into the body of Christ, all the corruption that is in us must be destroyed." –John Calvin, Calvin's Commentary on the Bible

Arminian Response: God is rich in mercy and was able to keep his Covenant intact, and yet deal with the faithful and unfaithful through grace.

Comment: Speaking of David's Dynasty "Thus the covenant could be conditional in any or more generations and yet be unconditional in its final outcome." –John MacArthur, *The MacArthur Study Bible*

Quick Points:

1) Sometimes love is manifested in discipline.

2) God's Covenant would be established, though some of the links in the process would prove to be impure and not partakers of godliness.

From the Experts:

"As the Lord corrected the posterity of David for their transgressions, so his people shall be corrected for their sins. Yet it is but a rod, not a sword; it is to correct, not to destroy. It is a rod in the hand of God, who is wise, and knows what he does; gracious, and will do what is best. It is a rod which they shall never feel, but when there is need. As the sun and moon remain in heaven, whatever changes there seem to be in them, and again appear in due season; so the covenant of grace made in Christ, whatever alteration seems to come to it, should not be questioned." –Matthew Henry, *Matthew Henry Concise Bible Commentary.*

The Bottom line: God would keep His promise of a dynasty for David and the Messiah, though not all links would benefit eternally.

Notes:

Psalm 106:8 (NIV)

[8] Yet he saved them for his name's sake, to make his mighty power known.

Context: Looking back on God's good and faithful example during the Israelites wilderness wanderings.

Calvinist View: God saved His people to preserve election of the select few.

Arminian Response: God saved His people to preserve the plan of salvation that would be freely offered to all willing souls.

Comment: If God was going to establish salvation history for the Messiah, it would take much grace & mercy. Mixed in with this was the tool He gave humans (freewill) that would need much grace, strong guidance, and at times nudging.

Quick Points:

1) Salvation history has order and planning to it.

2) All salvation is for the Glory of God.

3) God chose the Hebrew nation to work salvation history through. He would work through willing souls that responded by faith to the godly path.

The Bottom line: God acted out of love and mercy to the undeserving at times, and preserved His line of the Messiah in Israel for salvation.

Notes:

Psalm 106:46 (NIV)

[46] He caused them to be pitied by all who held them captive.

Context: Looking back on God's good and faithful example during the Israelites wilderness wanderings.

Calvinist View: God sovereignly made the Egyptians to gift the Israelites before leaving Egypt.

Arminian Response: God fulfilled His purpose of salvation, by equipping the Israelites to be able to furnish the Tabernacle and begin worship of Yahweh.

Comment: God allowed the Israelites to receive favor as they left Egypt, but this was not the only time. "The prime example of the Israelite exiles being pitied by their captors is the decree of Cyrus allowing their release and return." –*The Wesley Bible*

This was a carrying out purpose in His salvation history, nudging people and things that needed to be in the right place, but not overriding freewill.

Quick Points:

1) This was God graciously blessing His people, preparing them materially for equipping the Tabernacle by gifts.

2) This is not an overriding of freewill, but ordaining the path of salvation history to take shape.

From the Experts:

"He gave Israel favor in the eyes of her captors." –*The Dake Annotated Reference Bible*

The Bottom line: For the promotion of His honor and glory; that it might be seen that he is powerful and merciful." – Albert Barnes, *Barnes' Notes on the Whole Bible*

Notes:

Psalm 115:3 (NIV)

[3] Our God is in heaven; he does whatever pleases him.

Context: The True God versus idols and false gods.

Calvinist View: God raises people to election and others to damnation to His pleasure.

Arminian Response: God answers to no one, but does not act part from love, mercy, and holiness. He is not the author of evil.

Comment: Idols can only be worshipped, but cannot respond themselves. God is above all and yet allows humans to experience His great love.

Quick Points:

1) God can do whatever He pleases.

2) God always acts out of love and holiness.

3) There are certain things God has chosen not to do (evil, sin).

From the Experts:

"In heaven suggests a contrast between God and the earthbound idols." –*The Wesley Bible*

The Bottom line: Only God does what He pleases and yet is loving at all times.

Notes:

Psalm 135:6 (NIV)
⁶ The LORD does whatever pleases him, in the heavens and on the earth, in the seas and all their depths.

Context: God mighty in Creation- uncontested by false gods.

Calvinist View: God interacts as He pleases with sinner and saint.

Arminian Response: It pleases God to offer salvation to sinners and knows who will be saved. He is not pleased with giving people no options.

Comment: The God, who did not need sacrifices (Ps. 50) to be God, was Ruler of the whole Earth. This is a panoramic look at God and what He does and is. He is unchallenged and answerable to none, yet He does not act against His holiness and love, in regards to humans. This does not mean He damns souls based on an ordinance from long ago, but by laws judging sin.

Quick Points:

1) The Creator rules the created.

2) He only does good.

3) He allows evil to be chosen by free agents, but does not instigate it.

The Bottom line: This is not reckless license to sin, but a reminder that God is Almighty.

Notes:

Proverbs 16:4 (NIV)
⁴ The LORD works out everything for his own ends- even the wicked for a day of disaster.

Context: Wisdom and God's Care

Calvinist View: The wicked are set for an election of judgment.

Arminian Response: The judgment of the wicked is known beforehand, but brought about by personal sin.

Comment: God operates on God's time, and is "just" to do so. The Scripture says "the wicked for a day of disaster" not: "He makes them wicked for a day of disaster."

Quick Points:

1) God works out the end of the wicked, but does not originate wickedness (make the wicked wicked).

2) Personal sin leads to disaster.

From the Experts:

"He has reserved the wicked for the day when he shall receive his well-deserved punishment." –*The Dake Annotated Reference Bible*

The Bottom line: God is right to act as God and judge the unrepentant sinner.

Notes:

Proverbs 19:21 (NIV)
[21] Many are the plans in a man's heart, but it is the LORD's purpose that prevails.

Context: Solomon's Proverbs: Synthesized Thoughts / King and Court

Calvinist View: The Lord makes His decreed plans reality.

Arminian Response: The Lord works His plans out and reminds free humans that He is God.

Comment: Only God's purpose is guaranteed to prevail. He does not force His way on humans, though He could. He does fulfill His eternal purposes through the arena of freewill.

Quick Points:

1) No one but God can guarantee the end of one's planning.

2) Freewill is using a God-given gift for good or evil.

3) God's purpose can be achieved through His process of freewill in humans.

From the Experts:

"The heart of the natural man has many schemes, but only those plans that are worked in harmony with the will of God will stand." –*The Dake Annotated Reference Bible*

The Bottom line: All human effort needs to be God-led, including freewill.

Notes:

Isaiah 10:5-13 (NIV)
[5] "Woe to the Assyrian, the rod of my anger, in whose hand is the club of my wrath!
[6] I send him against a godless nation, I dispatch him against a people who anger me, to seize loot and snatch plunder, and to trample them down like mud in the streets.
[7] But this is not what he intends, this is not what he has in mind; his purpose is to destroy, to put an end to many nations.

[12] When the Lord has finished all his work against Mount Zion and Jerusalem, he will say, "I will punish the king of Assyria for the willful pride of his heart and the haughty look in his eyes.

Context: Hope for the Future and the Impending Assyrian Invasion.

Calvinist View: Assyria was raised for election of judgment.

Arminian Response: Assyria had her day of judgment for sins after being used by God for His purpose.

Comment: Assyria was used by God to punish sin– even in Israel. God would ultimately punish Assyria for its pride and sin. This would be a righteous judgment.

Quick Points:

1) God uses anyone and anything for His purpose.

2) Assyria was pagan and wicked by choice.

3) God used them for His purpose, but then punished them for their personal sins (which He could not do in fairness if He made them wicked).

From the Experts:

"Assyria is the power which Jehovah is using for the punishment of His people, but because it fails to understand its true relation to God, it, in turn, will be judged." – G. Campbell Morgan, *An Exposition of the Whole Bible*

The Bottom line: While God can use anyone or anything to achieve His purpose, this does not delete freedom of human will (He has given).

Notes:

Isaiah 25:1 (NIV)

[1] O LORD, you are my God; I will exalt you and praise your name, for in perfect faithfulness you have done marvelous things, things planned long ago.

Context: Eschatological Feast on Mount Zion

Calvinist View: God planned the destiny of every human long ago.

Arminian Response: God planned for His purpose to be moved along through freedom granted to humans.

Comment: God has eternal plans and principles that govern time and space. They are not divorced from His holy, loving character. God does not sacrifice human life and soul to fulfill a mere plan (election to damnation) that would violate His own Laws and Person.

Quick Points:

1) God has planned out all things (including freewill)

2) He knows how freewill will play out.

The Bottom line: God planned long ago for salvation history, not unwarranted destruction of souls.

Notes:

Isaiah 45:22 (NIV)

[22] "Turn to me and be saved, all you ends of the earth; for I am God, and there is no other.

Context: Yahweh's Use of Cyrus to Deliver.

Calvinist View: The elect will turn to God and be saved.

Arminian Response: God calls "whosoever" will hear and turn to His graceful call.

Comment: God's call to salvation is universal in scope, but limited only by rejection of His invitation. It would be a false appeal, if it was only crafted for a select few. The call is to all, the reception is by a few.

Quick Points:

1) The call to be saved is open to all.

2) If it were to a pre-selected few, it would have been stated.

From the Experts:

"Salvation is offered to all." –*The Wesley Bible*

The Bottom line: God genuinely calls all to salvation and is able to bless and love more deeply those who respond.

> **Notes:**

Isaiah 53:11 (NIV)

[11] After the suffering of his soul, he will see the light [of life] and be satisfied; by his knowledge my righteous servant will justify many, and he will bear their iniquities.

Context: Prophecy of the Messiah: Sin Bearing Servant.

Calvinist View: The many who are justified are the elect.

Arminian Response: The many who are justified experience this state by faith.

Comment: Many will be justified by Jesus Christ. Many. Who are the many? Those who believe. Those who comprise the elect. Who fill out the elect?

This may seem like splitting hairs, but "the many" are the elect by activation, not the elect by decree. God knows who will activate salvation by faith, through His grace. He just doesn't pre-pick to be partial to only one group.

Quick Points:

1) God doesn't single out only some for salvation.

2) The "many" are those who believe by faith.

3) It is a mixture of God knowing who will believe, appointing salvation for those who will believe, and allowing people to respond to His gracious invitation.

From the Experts:

"When we come to know Him through faith, He both declares, and makes, us righteous." –*The Wesley Bible*

The Bottom line: Simply put– whoever responds is justified!

Notes:

Jeremiah 1:5 (NIV)
[5] "Before I formed you in the womb I knew you, before you were born I set you apart; I appointed you as a prophet to the nations."

Context: Introduction to Book

Calvinist View: Sovereign decree set forth upon the life of Jeremiah.

Arminian Response: God picked key people throughout salvation history, knowing they would live their freedom to His end.

Comment: If God was to pull off salvation history, then He would need key people in key places. Enter Jeremiah. He was planned and picked, but free to decide to obey. God knew he would be godly, but did not make his servitude without freeness to choose God out of love.

Quick Points:

1) God planned for Jeremiah to accomplish a specific task– prophet.

2) He was set apart to play a role in salvation history.

3) Jeremiah was a free agent along the way.

From the Experts:

"In a few special cases it seems that God has exercised a more particular control, as in the birth of Jeremiah, Josiah, and Cyrus." –*The Dake Annotated Reference Bible*

The Bottom line: This is not overriding of freewill, but God establishing a network of key free agents.

Notes:

Jeremiah 10:23 (NIV)
[23] I know, O LORD, that a man's life is not his own; it is not for man to direct his steps.

Context: Oracles against idolatry

Calvinist View: All life is planned and structured by God, both good and evil.

Arminian Response: God directs both the righteous and wicked, but it is in accordance with the compass of freewill He has given them.

Comment: Since godly freewill is not acting on self, but using God's tool for good, it is not being an outlaw, but respecter of His Law.

Quick Points:

1) Life belongs to God (we are loaned it).

2) Freewill is not ours, but a tool loaned us.

3) God knows where your steps will take you, but does not make you step off the "narrow path."

The Bottom line: Man is equipped with a tool to use for or against God, according to His plan.

Notes:

Jeremiah 13:23 (NIV)

[23] Can the Ethiopian change his skin or the leopard its spots? Neither can you do good who are accustomed to doing evil.

Context: God's Covenant Broken

Calvinist View: This passage proves the setting of some humans under a set state of wickedness.

Arminian Response: The wicked that are set in their way have no desire to do good.

Comment: There is no question that all humans are born in sin (by nature). Such a nature is not God's plan for the final state of experiencing God on Earth. It is altered only by God and His Spirit (1 Thess. 5:23. 24).

Quick Points:

1) The natural default human setting is evil.

2) Basic human "goodness" is by God's grace (i.e. to be able to love, show kindness).

3) Moral goodness is a gracious spiritual gift

The Bottom line: No one is good based on his or her own personal merit (apart from God).

> **Notes:**

Daniel 4:34-35 (NIV)

[34] At the end of that time, I, Nebuchadnezzar, raised my eyes toward heaven, and my sanity was restored. Then I praised the Most High; I honored and glorified him who lives forever. His dominion is an eternal dominion; his kingdom endures from generation to generation.
[35] All the peoples of the earth are regarded as nothing. He does as he pleases with the powers of heaven and the peoples of the earth. No one can hold back his hand or say to him: "What have you done?"

Context: Nebuchadnezzar's Judgment (Madness)

Calvinist View: Strong sovereignty of God. "Lifted eyes" grace enables a person to do this." –John MacArthur, *The MacArthur Study Bible*

Arminian Response: No one can stand against God. Granted freedom is not standing against Him, but operating under Him.

Comment: Nebuchadnezzar was highlighting the omnipotence of God. He himself had benefitted from God's mercy.

Quick Points:

1) God is portrayed as Almighty.

2) The Almighty can still be Ultimate and yet impart freewill.

3) Nebuchadnezzar's sin was pride, which brought judgment

The Bottom line: God is All-Powerful, answerable to no one, but acts justly.

```
Notes:
```

Jonah 2:9 (NIV)
[9] But I, with a song of thanksgiving, will sacrifice to you. What I have vowed I will make good. Salvation comes from the LORD."

Context: Jonah Gives Thanks.

Calvinist View: Salvation comes from God as He lays it out on whom He plans.

Arminian Response: Salvation comes from God and is shared on humanity fairly.

Comment: Jonah was responding in like fashion of the ancient mariners, who offered sacrifices. As he was humbled, he saw God as He was– supreme. He experienced God's nudging and love.

Quick Points:

1) Salvation was planned by God.

2) It is offered through freewill, by God.

3) It is sustained by being "in Christ."

From the Experts:

"Salvation is the Lords"– It not only comes from Him, but also belongs to Him." –Merrill F. Unger, *Unger's Commentary on the Old Testament*

The Bottom line: From start to finish salvation is a God-thing.

Notes:

Malachi 3:7 (NIV)

[7] Ever since the time of your forefathers you have turned away from my decrees and have not kept them. <u>Return to me, and I will return to you," says the LORD Almighty</u>. "But you ask, 'How are we to return?' (Underlining added)

Context: The People's sin: robbing God

Calvinist View: This would be out of fellowship and returning to it; the elect would naturally return. "In light of that deep defection, the LORD issued a call to repentance." – Merrill F. Unger, *Unger's Commentary on the Old Testament*

Arminian Response: This is the heart that has wandered from and left God, and is called again by God to union.

Comment: Israel had wandered into sin and needed to be called to repentance. The Lord planned to bring His remnant back to Israel from captivity, though not all would be turned to God.

Quick Points:

1) The people were called by grace to return.

2) Then God would respond.

3) We see the importance of action on our part.

From the Experts:

"If you lose any degree of grace, seek to gain it at once and do not wait till you have lost more till you make a vigorous effort to regain it." –Bishop B.T. Roberts, *Holiness Teachings*

The Bottom line: God's promise to return to the repentant is not for just half the audience.

Notes:

Rightly Understanding Commonly Used (Calvinist/ Once Saved Always Saved) Proof Texts...

New Testament

Matthew 1:21 (NIV)

²¹ She will give birth to a son, and you are to give him the name Jesus, because he will save his people from their sins."

Context: Jesus' origin Divine and [Earthly: Mary].

Calvinist View: The "his people" refers to the elect set from eternity.

Arminian Response: Jesus came to save those who would believe, known to God.

Comment: His people were the Jews and beyond. He came to give everyone a chance, not just a few, but all.

Quick Points:

1) Jesus came to deal with sin.

2) It was for Jew & Gentile

3) God would touch all hearts, but not all would receive Him.

4) "Jesus" means Savior, which does not denote partially saving a pre-selected few.

From the Experts:

"The system could not produce Him. He came to crown the system and transform it. So came the KING, but His name was called JESUS, for the Kingdom had disintegrated and been devastated by sin, and He must begin by saving His people from their sins." –G. Campbell Morgan, *An Exposition of the Whole Bible*

The Bottom line: All who receive Christ are "His people."

Notes:

Matthew 7:18-20 (NIV)

[18] A good tree cannot bear bad fruit, and a bad tree cannot bear good fruit. [19] Every tree that does not bear good fruit is cut down and thrown into the fire. [20] Thus, by their fruit you will recognize them.

Context: Kingdom of Heaven Heirs

Calvinist View: This shows the two ways a person can go, the false way or true way: elect or non-elect.

Arminian Response: A person is defined by works that live out of true faith.

Comment: Works do not save, but good deeds do eventually show the nature of the heart. A bad tree (unbeliever) can fake the fruit of a good tree only so long, before the true colors shine through.

Quick Points:

1) Works (fruits) do not save but indicate the state of spiritual being.

2) Some fruits cannot be faked, while others can, but ultimately one's true colors come forth.

From the Experts:

"Jesus tells us that the moral quality of the life is the only true indication of the spiritual state of the heart." –Purkiser, *Security– The False & The True*

The Bottom line: Indicators of salvation are found reflecting on one's life.

Notes:

Matthew 7:21 (NIV)

[21] "Not everyone who says to me, 'Lord, Lord,' will enter the kingdom of heaven, but only he who does the will of my Father who is in heaven.

Context: Disciples: True and False

Calvinist View: "Jesus was not suggesting that works are meritorious for salvation, but that true faith will not fail to produce the fruit for good works." –John MacArthur, *The MacArthur Study Bible*

Arminian Response: Salvation faith and actions run parallel in the life of a true believer, out of love for God, not programmed response.

Comment: Not everyone who calls Jesus "Lord" or sees salvation more as a necklace or item than relationship "in Christ"– is saved. The doer is living out their faith and does not see it as separable from the person and presence of Christ in one's life. Eventually when faith ceases, salvation ebbs away.

Quick Points:

1) Many claim to be saved.

2) Actions prove faith.

3) Salvation is not merely by decree, but graciously through faith.

From the Experts:

"The sense of this verse seems to be this: No person, by merely acknowledging my authority, believing in the Divinity of my nature, professing faith in the perfection of my righteousness, and infinite merit of my atonement, shall enter into the kingdom of heaven—shall have any part with God in glory; but he who doeth the will of my Father—he who gets the bad tree rooted up, the good tree planted, and continues to bring forth fruit to the glory and praise of God. There is a good saying among the rabbis on this subject. "A man should be as vigorous as a panther, as swift as an eagle, as fleet as a stag, and as strong as a lion, to do the will of his Creator." –John Wesley, *A Commentary and Critical Notes*.

"Let us take heed of resting in outward privileges and doings, lest we deceive ourselves, and perish eternally, as multitudes do, with a lie in our right hand." –Matthew Henry, *Matthew Henry Concise Bible Commentary*.

The Bottom line: Freely doing God's will proves the genuine nature of one's salvation.

Notes:

Matthew 10:21-32 (NIV)

[24] "A student is not above his teacher, nor a servant above his master. [25] It is enough for the student to be like his teacher, and the servant like his master. If the head of the house has been called Beelzebub, how much more the members of his household! [26] "So do not be afraid of them. There is nothing concealed that will not be disclosed, or hidden that will not be made known. [28] Do not be afraid of those who kill the body but cannot kill the soul. Rather, be afraid of the One who can destroy both soul and body in hell. [31] So don't be afraid; you are worth more than many sparrows. [32] "Whoever acknowledges me before men, I will also acknowledge him before my Father in heaven.

Context: Kingdom of God Proclaimed

Calvinist View:

The elect will not abandon God, or be abandoned by Him. Their works are not necessary though to prove their eternally ordained faith.

"Christ employs the very powerful argument, that this frail and perishing lift ought to be little regarded by men who have been created for a heavenly immortality. The statement amounts to this, that if believers will consider for what purpose they were born, and what is their condition, they will have no reason to be so earnest in desiring an earthly life. But the words have still a richer and fuller meaning: for we are here taught by Christ that the fear of God is dead in those men who, through dread of tyrants, fall from a confession of their faith, and that a brutish stupidity reigns in the hearts of those who, through dread of death, do not hesitate to abandon that confession." –John Calvin, *Calvin's Commentary on the Bible*

Arminian Response: The believer that is believing fears God, and not humans who can only destroy the body.

Comment: The believer, who fears man instead of God, does not love or have true reverence for God. Such a person may have begun to be saved and was experiencing God's grace, but has not held firm in the face of adversity.

Quick Points:

1) Fearing (respecting) anything above God is not acceptable.

2) God judges those who do not live out their faith.

From the Experts:

"The Scriptures mean, by a profession of religion, an exhibition of it in every circumstance of the life, and before all men. It is not merely in *one* act that we must do it, but in every act. We must be ashamed neither of the person, the character, the doctrines, nor the requirements of Christ." –Albert Barnes, *Notes on the New Testament Explanatory and Practical.*

"Whosoever shall confess me - Publicly acknowledge me for the promised Messiah. But this confession implies the receiving his whole doctrine, Mark 8:38, and obeying all his commandments. Luke 9:26." –John Wesley, *Explanatory Notes upon the New Testament.*

The Bottom line: The Lord can destroy anyone who is unfaithful and rejects His grace.

Notes:

Matthew 11:27 (NIV)

27 "All things have been committed to me by my Father. No one knows the Son except the Father, and no one knows the Father except the Son and those to whom the Son chooses to reveal him.

Context: Questions and Opposition to Jesus and the Kingdom.

Calvinist View: The Son reveals the father to the elect.

Arminian Response: A standing invitation is extended to anyone who believes.

Comment: God the Father and Son work together and carried out salvation perfectly to humanity. No one comes to the Father but by the Son, the Door, and that is by faith not pre-election of a few.

Quick Points:

1) No one comes to the Father but by the Son.

2) Faith draws the souls to Christ, not pre-selection.

From the Experts:

"Christ invites all to come to him for rest to their souls. He alone gives this invitation; men come to him, when, feeling their guilt and misery, and believing his love and power to help, they seek him in fervent prayer. Thus it is the duty and interest of weary and heavy-laden sinners, to come to Jesus Christ." –Matthew Henry, *Matthew Henry Concise Bible Commentary*.

"...Scriptures that urge all men to come to God and to Christ without any mention of the Father's drawing. Here is a partial list: Deuteronomy 30:2; 1 Samuel 7:3; Nehemiah 1:9; Isaiah 55:1-7; Hosea 6:1; Zechariah 1:3; Matthew 11:28; 19:14; Mark 10:14; Luke 18:16; John 7:37; Hebrews 11:6; Revelation 22:17." –Dave Hunt, *Debating Calvinism*

The Bottom line: The Son reveals the Father to those who seek Him.

Notes:

Matthew 20:28 (NIV)

[28] just as the Son of Man did not come to be served, but to serve, and to give his life as a ransom for many."

Context: Jesus Received and Rejected (Jerusalem).

Calvinist View: For the many who were destined to receive salvation (elect).

"*All* in Scripture is often limited to kinds and classes, *many* never means all." –James White, *Debating Calvinism*

Arminian Response: The "many" refers to all who would walk the Earth, though not all will believe.

Comment: Who are the "many" spoken of? Those who believe Christ at His Word. Those who were allowed by God in ages past to be part of the believers freely.

Quick Points:

1) Jesus gave His life for "many."

2) Those who believe are "elect," but the invite is truly for all.

3) Jesus truly gave His life for all who would believe. He knew who would believe, but died out of love for all.

From the Experts:

"It is a sacrifice for the sins of men, and is that true and substantial sacrifice, which those of the law faintly and imperfectly represented. It was a ransom for many, enough for all, working upon many; and, if for many, then the poor trembling soul may say, Why not for me?" –Matthew Henry, *Matthew Henry Concise Bible Commentary.*

"For many" See also Matthew 26:28, John 10:16, 1 Timothy 2:6, 1 John 2:2 2 Corinthians 5:14,15, Hebrews 2:9." –Albert Barnes, *Notes on the New Testament Explanatory and Practical.*

The Bottom line: God's mercy through Jesus is for the crowd, not just the few who believe.

Notes:

Matthew 22:14 (NIV)
[14] "For many are invited, but few are chosen."

Context: Jesus Received and Rejected (Jerusalem).

Calvinist View: Chosen refers to a previous action by God in eternity past– choosing who would be righteous.

"Those who have been predestined experience the results of that eternal action in time. God calls them into relationship with Jesus." –James White, *Debating Calvinism.*

Arminian Response: Chosen refers to those who take God up on His invitation, and activate what has been planned for them.

Comment: Everyone is issued an invitation to salvation, but not all respond. Those who respond, being in the minority, take hold of the chosen status set up for believers. It is not a choosing beforehand of a few, but a chosen beforehand of all who will respond, and God knows who they will be.

Quick Points:

1) As many as could be found were invited.

2) "Proper clothes"= spiritual fruit.

3) The chosen are the invited that obey God and reflect true obedience.

The Bottom line: Chosen constitutes accepting God's call, not having the right number.

> **Notes:**

Matthew 25:14-30 (Read passage)

The parable/ story of the Talents.

Context: Jesus' Final Conflicts with Religious Leaders

Calvinist View: The servants who were faithful were Elect.

Arminian Response: Being faithful is a characteristic of the Elect.

Comment: Does fruitfulness matter? This parable leans that direction. The servant that was not fruitful, didn't just get a slap on the hand, but was thrown into darkness "outside." Fruitfulness doesn't save, but is a characteristic of the "saved."

Quick Points:

1) Salvation is an investment from God.

2) Those who live out their salvation and reinvest it and reap dividends please God.

3) Those who do not obey God and work on being fruitful will not enjoy salvation forever.

From the Experts:

"The professed followers of Jesus include those who turn out to be unfaithful and who will have no share in the coming kingdom. It may be that they never believed or that they lapsed from belief…" –I. Howard Marshall, *Kept by the Power of God*

The Bottom line: The Elect are faithful and free to be so.

> **Notes:**

Mark 13:13 (NIV)
[13] All men will hate you because of me, but he who stands firm to the end will be saved.

Context: The Testing of the Servant

Calvinist View:

The elect stand firm because of their state and calling decreed by God.

"We ought to keep in remembrance what I formerly mentioned, that those who insist on explaining, with exactness, every minute phrase, are mistaken. The true meaning is, though slothful and unprofitable servants are now endued with the gifts of the Spirit, yet they will at length be deprived of them all, that their wretched and shameful poverty may redound to the glory of the good." –John Calvin, *Calvin's Commentary on the Bible*

Arminian Response: The Christian standing firm to the end does so by continual faith and in the power of the grace of God. Their works prove their faith, resulting in reaching the finish line.

Comment: Everyone has a limit. God knows this and has supplied His grace to meet us in trials and tribulations (1 Corinthians 10:13). The Christian is not called to always survive in this life, but to be faithful and overcome in Christ. Those who do not, do not please Christ.

Quick Points:

1) Persecution comes to the believer.

2) Enduring it is rooted in the grace of God.

3) Failure is not making use of God's grace and power, and not the path of salvation ultimately.

From the Experts:

"We find here, therefore, a clear presentation of the paradox of the promise of divine protection and the demand for human faith and steadfastness. His faith is thus not a human achievement…but a continuing trust in God. But neither is this faith to be regarded as something given by God independently of human volition." –I. Howard Marshall, *Kept by the Power of God*

The Bottom line: Enduring to the end (taking hold of salvation) is rooted in God and His grace.

Notes:

Mark 13:22 (NIV)

[22] For false Christs and false prophets will appear and perform signs and miracles to deceive the elect– if that were possible.

Context: Testing of the Servant

Calvinist View: It is not possible since the Elect are eternally secure.

Arminian Response: Elect is the blessing of standing in salvation, and even such can be tempted.

Comment: This verse is looking at God protecting the elect that are in a right standing with God, by giving them the knowledge/ guidance to not be deceived. This is not a verse stating that the elect cannot fall prey or sin, because they are elect.

Quick Points:

1) Election is standing in salvation.

2) Even such can be tempted.

3) It is possible apart from God's protecting.

From the Experts:

"…the word eklektos (elect) does not contain in itself the certainty of perseverance. The idea of election as such does not exclude the possibility of apostasy." –I. Howard Marshall, *Kept by the Power of God*

The Bottom line: God takes care of His own, but they still have freewill to choose or deny Him.

Notes:

Luke 19:10 (NIV)

[10] For the Son of Man came to seek and to save what was lost."

Context: Zacchaeus Converted.

Calvinist View: This can only refer to the lost elect that are destined to be saved.

Arminian Response: This refers to those who are without Christ, who can be saved by faith.

Comment: God sent Jesus for the lost, not just the "elect-lost."

Quick Points:

1) Jesus came to bring salvation.

2) His scope was for all.

3) He can only save those realizing their lostness and need of a Savior– such are the elect.

From the Experts:

"They did not come looking for Him– He sought them. He went where people hurt and suffered so He could change their lives. His ministry clearly pictures God reaching out to find His lost children." –Frank Moore, *More Coffee Shop Theology*

The Bottom line: Jesus died for all the lost, though not all will receive Him.

Notes:

John 1:12-13 (NIV)

[12] Yet to all who received him, to those who believed in his name, he gave the right to become children of God– [13] children born not of natural descent, nor of human decision or a husband's will, but born of God.

Context: Jesus the Eternal Word of God (Dwelling in Human Flesh)

Calvinist View: "Given the right" refers to the determining factor of salvation.

Arminian Response: Those who believed were given the right, not those who were pre-categorized.

Comment: It all starts with receiving Christ as Lord. Such who believe children of God– become born again. This is not their idea, but God's, who gave freewill to be exercised. Notice the pattern: Humans responding to (prevenient) grace, the right given to become a child of God, born of God; not decreed to be saved and then believed after the fact.

Quick Points:

1) The status of being "child of God" is based on believing in Christ.

2) Becoming a child of God is from responding to God's call (not mere human determination).

3) It is according to the plan of God: call, grace, gift.

From the Experts:

"**But as many as received him** – Jews or Gentiles; **that believe on his name** – That is, on him. The moment they believe, they are sons; and because they are sons, God sendeth forth the Spirit of his Son into their hearts, crying, Abba, Father. –John Wesley, *Explanatory Notes upon the New Testament.*

The Bottom line: All who receive Christ are saved and become children of God.

Notes:

John 6:37 (NIV)
[37] All that the Father gives me will come to me, and whoever comes to me I will never drive away.

Context: Jesus Instructing His Listeners (Disciples, etc.)

Calvinist View: This passage shows election of the saved as well as security. Irresistible grace.

"Again, we infer, that God works in his elect by such an efficacy of the Holy Spirit, that not one of them falls away." –John Calvin, *Calvin's Commentaries on the Whole Bible*

Arminian Response: God's grace is successful in drawing. God does not drive sinners away, the drive and desire of sin does.

Comment: The action in the text is that of the Father giving Jesus souls for salvation, and Jesus not trying to tempt or get rid of those who have believed. Freewill is also in the picture: The Father having given them, Jesus loving and protecting, and the human still having freewill to choose or deny God.

Quick Points:

1) God the Father allows those who believe to come to Him (and Jesus).

2) This is part of the logistics of salvation, which also includes freewill.

From the Experts:

"This action is not opposed to human freedom…It is that hunger and thirst after righteousness (Matt: 5:6) which the preparatory action of the Father produces in sincere souls. Every time Jesus sees such a soul coming to Him, He receives it as a gift of God, and His success with it is certain." –Frederick L. Godet

All that the Father giveth me – All that feel themselves lost, and follow the drawings of the Father, he in a peculiar manner giveth to the Son: **I will in nowise cast out** – I will give him pardon, holiness, and heaven,

If he endure to the end – to rejoice in his light. –John Wesley, *Explanatory Notes upon the New Testament.*

The Bottom line: God is proficient in drawing and securing free humans.

Notes:

John 6:44 (NIV)
[44] "No one can come to me unless the Father who sent me draws him, and I will raise him up at the last day.

Context: Jesus and His Critics

Calvinist View: "No one can come to me" (Total Depravity); "the father…draws him" (Unconditional election); "No one…" (Limited Atonement/ Double Predestination).

"…therefore that faith does not depend on the will of men, but that it is God who gives it." –John Calvin, *Calvin's Commentaries on the Bible*

Arminian Response: The Father draws souls to Jesus period. That is the process in coming to God. Humans are unable to approach God, without a prevenient graceful drawing.

Comment: No one can just walk up to God to follow Him. The Father draws humans to Christ. This is not based on being raised in the church or having a certain nationality (Jewish) or ancestor, but based on God. God draws all (knowing who will respond), but does not prevent people from coming. Sin and selfish desires draw one away from God.

Quick Points:

1) God's grace allows humans' access to God.

2) Freewill is not outside of this equation, but inside it.

3) Free humans respond to God's drawing and are saved.

From the Experts:

"The God who sends Jesus for souls, on the other hand, draws souls to Jesus." –Frederick L. Godet

"No man can believe in Christ, unless God give him power: he draws us first, by good desires. Not by compulsion, not by laying the will under any necessity; but by the strong and sweet, yet still resistible, motions of his heavenly grace." –John Wesley, Explanatory Notes on the NT

"Unless God thus draw, no man will ever come to Christ; because none could, without this drawing, ever feel the need of a Savior." –Adam Clarke, *A Commentary and Critical Notes*.

"Christ repeatedly calls all to believe on Him." –Dave Hunt, *Debating Calvinism*

"The very desire we have to find God comes from His drawing influence on our lives." –Frank Moore, *More Coffee Shop Theology*

The Bottom line: God draws by grace enabling peopple to believe.

Notes:

John 8:31-34 (NIV)

[31] To the Jews who had believed him, Jesus said, "If you hold to my teaching, you are really my disciples. [32] Then you will know the truth, and the truth will set you free." [33] They answered him, "We are Abraham's descendants and have never been slaves of anyone. How can you say that we shall be set free?" [34] Jesus replied, "I tell you the truth, everyone who sins is a slave to sin.

Context: Feast of Tabernacles/ Spiritual Freedom

Calvinist View: The elect hold what they have been eternally called to.

"He exhorts to perseverance in the faith those who have tasted of his doctrine." –John Calvin, *Calvin's Commentaries on the Bible*

Arminian Response: These disciples bear fruit in accordance with Christ's teachings.

Comment: Believers hold to the teachings of Christ and do not live as slaves to sin. If they realize or are made aware of sin, like David, they confess their sins to their Advocate, Jesus (1 John 2:1).

Quick Points:

1) Discipleship proves itself to be true by fruit.

2) Holding to the teachings of Christ is not optional.

From the Experts:

"To "abide" is compared to a fertile soil in which true faith must be rooted ever more deeply in order to thrive and bear fruit." –Frederick L. Godet

It is not enough to receive God's truth—we must retain and walk in it. And it is only when we receive the truth, love it, keep it, and walk in it, that we are the genuine disciples of Christ. –Adam Clarke, *A Commentary and Critical Notes.*

"He that committeth sin, is, in fact, the slave of sin." –Wesley, *Explanatory Notes on NT*

The Bottom line: True disciples obey God.

> Notes:

John 8:42-47 (NIV)

[42] Jesus said to them, "If God were your Father, you would love me, for I came from God and now am here. I have not come on my own; but he sent me.

[43] Why is my language not clear to you? Because you are unable to hear what I say.

[44] You belong to your father, the devil, and you want to carry out your father's desire. He was a murderer from the beginning, not holding to the truth, for there is no truth in him. When he lies, he speaks his native language, for he is a liar and the father of lies.

[45] Yet because I tell the truth, you do not believe me!

[46] Can any of you prove me guilty of sin? If I am telling the truth, why don't you believe me?

[47] He who belongs to God hears what God says. The reason you do not hear is that you do not belong to God."

Context: Feast of Tabernacles/ Spiritual Freedom

Calvinist View: The elect hear because God has opened their ears through election in eternity past.

Arminian Response: Grace opens the heart and person to Christ.

Comment: Believers are naturally filled with the love of the Father. The religious leaders proved they were "of the Devil" as they were filed with hate. The way you love reflects your experience (or lack of) with God.

Quick Points:

1) Inability to hear God is due to evil desires, not God.

2) Those who belong to and love God listen to Him.

From the Experts:

"To be of God…implies the free determination of the man."–Frederick. L. Godet

"But Jesus regarded their perdition as yet contingent: "if you believe not that I am he, you shall die in your sins" (v.24)." –Robert Shank, *Elect in the Son*

The Bottom line: Those who belong to God listen to God.

Notes:

When Arminian theologians go "bad"...

John 10:11-15 (NIV)

[11] "I am the good shepherd. The good shepherd lays down his life for the sheep.

[12] The hired hand is not the shepherd who owns the sheep. So when he sees the wolf coming, he abandons the sheep and runs away. Then the wolf attacks the flock and scatters it.

[13] The man runs away because he is a hired hand and cares nothing for the sheep.

[14] "I am the good shepherd; I know my sheep and my sheep know me-

[15] just as the Father knows me and I know the Father-and I lay down my life for the sheep.

Context: Feast of Tabernacles/ Spiritual Freedom

Calvinist View: The sheep are the elect, who know Jesus, though the calling is not tied to works.

Arminian Response: The sheep know and are known by Jesus. Kind of hard to have such an intimate fellowship rebelling and sitting on the porch of sin.

Comment: To be known by Christ is by close personal fellowship. Jesus knows the Father in such a manner, so then it seems foolish to expect to be considered a sheep if such a relationship is missing.

Quick Points:

1) Jesus knows the sheep/ the sheep know Jesus.

2) "Knowing" is the same, as Jesus knows the Father.

3) Intimate fellowship, not salvation apart from fellowship.

From the Experts:

"They know me as their father, protector, and Savior; they acknowledge me and my truth before the world; and they approve of me, my word, my ordinances, and my people, and manifest this by their attachment to me, and their zeal for my glory." –Adam Clarke, *A Commentary and Critical Notes.*

The Bottom line: True sheep know God by close fellowship and obedience, just as the Father and Son interract.

Notes:

John 10:25-26 (NIV)

[25] Jesus answered, "I did tell you, but you do not believe. The miracles I do in my Father's name speak for me,

[26] but you do not believe because you are not my sheep.

Context: Teaching on Unity of God

Calvinist View: They cannot believe because they are not elect, and cannot believe.

"Those whom God does not look must always continue to look away from him." –John Calvin, *Calvin's Commentaries on the Bible*

Arminian Response: Unbelief is a sign of personal sin, not God determining people to this end.

Comment: God's sheep hear His voice (obey). Unbelief and rebellion led the religious leaders in a path away from Jesus and God. It does the same today.

Quick Points:

1) God shares His Truth but many do not believe.

2) God's grace enables people to believe.

3) If you do not believe, you are not His sheep (even if you think you are elect).

From the Experts:

"That there unbelief did not derive from some eternal, irrevocable decree of God is evident from the fact that to the same man Jesus appealed, "believe [my] works, that you may know and believe that the Father is in me, and I in him" (v.38). –Robert Shank, *Elect in the Son*

The Bottom line: Belief is an undeniable mark of a believer.

Notes:

John 10:27-29 (NIV)
[27] My sheep listen to my voice; I know them, and they follow me.
[28] I give them eternal life, and they shall never perish; no one can snatch them out of my hand.
[29] My Father, who has given them to me, is greater than all; no one can snatch them out of my Father's hand.

Context: The Feast of Dedication/ Opposition to Jesus' Teaching

Calvinist View: The sheep are elect and secure eternally.

"For God effectually calls all whom he has elected. So that the sheep of Christ are proved by their faith." –John Calvin, *Calvin's Commentaries on the Bible*

Arminian Response: These prove they are sheep by obeying, defining their faith, and are thus secure.

Comment: God's sheep (Believers) are secure. What constitutes a believer? Is a reckless lifestyle of sin after salvation an issue?

Is "snatching" backsliding to apostasy? Is this passage looking to the Believer who is believing, or the professing Believer whose loyalties have changed, whose fruit are questionable?

Quick Points:

1) These sheep: listen, know, and follow.

2) Of such eternal life is secure.

3) One cannot have security and yet omit the first three (listen, know, follow).

From the Experts:

"To those whom I know truly love Me "shall never perish," provided they abide in My love. Those who follow Me, neither men nor devils can pluck out of My hand." (Wesley in *The Wesley Bible*)

"Let no man for the sake of a false security deny the plain statement of God's Word– "My sheep...follow Me." There are no exceptions allowed. He who does not follow is not of Christ's fold no matter how loudly he may bleat his "ba-a-a's." –Purkiser, *Security– the False & The True*

The Bottom line: Sheep obey God and are secure, not just bear the name.

John 12:32 (NIV)

[32] But I, when I am lifted up from the earth, will draw all men to myself."

Context: Jesus as Redeemer of the World

Calvinist View: Draw is a picture of Sovereign determinism.

Arminian Response: Jesus would open the way of salvation to be offered to all, and wrap His loving arms around those who believe.

Comment: Jesus provided salvation for all, though not all would make use of it. Jesus did not just draw the selected ones.

Quick Points:

1) Jesus provided salvation with everyone in mind.

2) His love drew Judas a betrayer to His side, even though He knew His heart and the outcome.

From the Experts:

"Gentiles as well as Jews. And those who follow my drawings, Satan shall not be able to keep." –John Wesley, *Explanatory Notes upon the New Testament.*

The Bottom line: Salvations recruiting power graciously is given to all.

> ### Notes:

John 12:39-40 (NIV)

[39] For this reason they could not believe, because, as Isaiah says elsewhere: [40] "He has blinded their eyes and deadened their hearts, so they can neither see with their eyes, nor understand with their hearts, nor turn-and I would heal them."

Context: The continued unbelief of the Jews

Calvinist View: These people, as in Isaiah's day, were never meant to "see" and be saved. It was God's purpose and plan to do this.

"It is certain that all would continue to be such by nature, if the Lord did not form to obedience to him those whom he has elected," –John Calvin, *Calvin's Commentaries on the Bible*

Arminian Response: This was a reinforcing what was already at work in hearts. "For this reason" points back to their denial of the Lord's miracles and message. God does not blind people spiritually to categorize them, but categorizes those who have blinded themselves by sin.

Comment: Blindness of spirit comes from hardness of heart, not a hardening by God.

Quick Points:

1) Jesus (and Isaiah) were addressing dealing with sinners who were hardened.

2) God would not have hardened them, apart from deserving judgment.

3) This is not persons set aside for the category of evil, apart from personal action.

From the Experts:

"If all men have this "inability" to believe, why would God blind them and prevent them from believing?" –Dave Hunt, *Debating Calvinism*

The Bottom line: Unrepentant sin hardens hearts, not instigation by God.

Notes:

John 15:16 (NIV)

[16] You did not choose me, but I chose you and appointed you to go and bear fruit-fruit that will last. Then the Father will give you whatever you ask in my name.

Context: The Importance of Abiding and Fruit Bearing

Calvinist View: Human choice is not in the picture, this is unconditional election.

"A man is not moved of his own accord to seek Christ, until he has been sought by him." –John Calvin, *Calvin's Commentaries on the Bible*

Arminian Response: The choosing here was to discipleship and to bear fruit, not salvation.

Comment: God has always been planning salvation for us "before" we were ready. He supplied the grace that can move us. He draws sinners. He chooses us always before. This isn't however a choosing to divide, but choose to allow souls to His salvation through Jesus.

Quick Points:

1) God chooses all humanity to receive salvation.

2) Chosen to be saved then bear fruit.

From the Experts:

"You are chosen and ordained to: 1) Go and produce fruit (v.15); 2) Produce eternal works (v.15); 3) Get an answer to every prayer (v.15)." –*The Dake Annotated Reference Bible*

"The choice of which Christ speaks is to the apostolate rather than to salvation (Mk. 3:13; Lk. 6:13; Acts 1:2), a choice which Christ made among His larger body of disciples (Lk. 6:13)." –Robert Shank, *Elect in the Son*

The Bottom line: God chooses disciples by grace to be fruitful, not mere name bearers.

Notes:

John 17:1-6 (NIV)
[1] After Jesus said this, he looked toward heaven and prayed: "Father, the time has come. Glorify your Son, that your Son may glorify you.
[2] For you granted him authority over all people that he might give eternal life to all those you have given him.
[3] Now this is eternal life: that they may know you, the only true God, and Jesus Christ, whom you have sent.
[4] I have brought you glory on earth by completing the work you gave me to do.
[5] And now, Father, glorify me in your presence with the glory I had with you before the world began.

[6] "I have revealed you to those whom you gave me out of the world. They were yours; you gave them to me and they have obeyed your word.

Context: Jesus Opposes Religious Community (Pharisees)

Calvinist View: The elect are given to the Son by the Father.

Arminian Response: Souls coming to Christ do so via the power of the Father.

Comment: Who are those given to Christ, a determined "no response required" elect? No. Those who God knew would respond by faith, not made to believe.

Quick Points:

1) All who will believe do so by the Father's approval.

2) Grace draws them from the world to God.

3) They obey the word of God.

From the Experts:

"Giveth me"– By giving them faith in what I have spoken (17:9)." –Wesley, *Explanatory Notes on the NT*

The Bottom line: Salvation, including freewill, is from God start to finish.

Notes:

John 17:3 (NIV)
[3] Now this is eternal life: that they may know you, the only true God, and Jesus Christ, whom you have sent.

Context: Jesus Opposes Religious Community (Pharisees)

Calvinist View: This knowing comes by Divine decree.

Arminian Response: This knowing comes by faith in Christ, through grace.

Comment: Does this mean that the Believer can never (not have) eternal life, never use God-given freewill to wander from a saving state? Or is this text simply stating what eternal life is, to those who know God and His Son, Jesus?

Quick Points:

1) "Eternal Life" describes the quality and duration of this life (in of itself).

2) It is not affected by humans who may start and yet cease to believe.

3) Since it is from the eternal God, it will always be eternal despite human interaction.

The Bottom line: Being in the state of knowing God brings eternal life.

Notes:

John 17:9 (NIV)
[9] I pray for them. I am not praying for the world, but for those you have given me, for they are yours.

Context: Jesus Opposes Religious Community (Pharisees)

Calvinist View: Jesus did not pray for the world, as it was non-elect.

"Now, Christ expressly declares that they who are given to him belong to the Father, and it is certain that they are given so as to believe, and that faith flows from this act of giving." –John Calvin, *Calvin's Commentaries on the Bible*

Arminian Response: Jesus is praying categorically: believers here, the world elsewhere.

Comment: It is ridiculous to believe for even a minute that Jesus was purposefully NOT praying for a large group of the human race here. Jesus prayer here is broken into categories simply as sections, not partitioning off His love for only a select few.

Quick Points:

1) The focus here is for believers.

2) Jesus does pray for the world (17:21, 23)

From the Experts:

"Christ's prayer is for believers (17:20), and would be inappropriate for the world of unbelievers, but that does not limit who can believe." –Dave Hunt, *Debating Calvinism*

"Although the burden of our Lord's prayer for the moment was for the Apostles, His concern went beyond them to include all who would believe through their word (v.20) and extended to all the world (that the world may believe and know, vs. 21, 23), a world for whose life He soon would give His flesh in sacrifice (6:51), being nailed to His cross and lifted up to die, that He might draw all men to Himself (12:32)." –Robert Shank, *Elect in the Son*

The Bottom line: John 17 is focused prayer, not praying with prejudice, but for the believers.

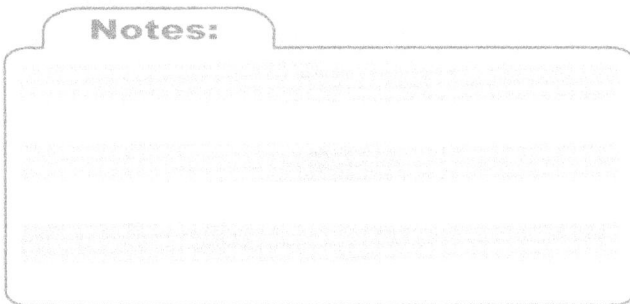

> **Notes:**

Acts 1:25 (NIV)
[25] to take over this apostolic ministry, which Judas left to go where he belongs."

Context: The choosing of Matthias

Calvinist View: Judas was called to betray and not be found among the elect. He was never saved. "The choosing of Judas was to apostleship and to the role of His betrayer." –James White, *Debating Calvinism*

Arminian Response: Judas experienced the grace of God, began to "follow" Christ, but never sold out, and died in his sins.

Comment: Judas is a good picture of the believer that experiences the grace of God tugging at your heart, but doesn't go deep. That He followed Jesus was a sign of initial commitment, but signs popped up of his evil heart: stealing from the disciples monies, concerned with monies that could have been given to the group but were spent on expensive perfume to anoint Jesus (Jn. 12:5), conspiring with the religious leaders against Jesus (Mt. 26:14), etc.

From the Experts:

"We believe the case of Judas is an instance of true apostasy, rather than of original and prolonged imposture. The statement that Judas "fell away" (Acts 1:25) from his ministry and apostleship is an assertion that, by a specific action, he disqualified himself. The necessary corollary is that he previously was qualified. The case of Judas, then, was one of apostasy, rather than original hypocrisy." –Robert Shank, *Life in the Son*

Bottom line: Judas went to perdition (damnation) by choices made.

Notes:

Acts 11:21-23 (NIV)

[21] The Lord's hand was with them, and a great number of people believed and turned to the Lord.
[22] News of this reached the ears of the church at Jerusalem, and they sent Barnabas to Antioch.
[23] When he arrived and saw the evidence of the grace of God, he was glad and encouraged them all to remain true to the Lord with all their hearts.

Context: The Disciples are Called Christians.

Calvinist View: A great number believed because God enabled them as the elect.

Arminian Response: A great number believed by faith, responding by turning to the Lord.

Comment: The word of God is a great salesman, drawing souls. God doesn't need to subdivide souls in pre-planned categories to make His plan work.

The Gospel is powerful, it reaches souls (whom) God knows who will respond, but they are free to respond. God fills out the elect by sharing the welcoming Gospel of Christ, and reeling in the catch.

Quick Points:

1) The Lord drew open hearts.

2) They were drawn into the elect category as the believed.

From the Experts:

"And the hand of the Lord – That is, the power of his Spirit." –John Wesley, *Explanatory Notes upon the New Testament*

"The meaning is, that God showed them favour, and evinced (revealed) his power in the conversion of their hearers." –Albert Barnes, *Notes on the New Testament Explanatory and Practical*

The Bottom line: Grace drew open hearts to salvation.

Notes:

Acts 13:48 (NIV)

[48] When the Gentiles heard this, they were glad and honored the word of the Lord; and all who were appointed for eternal life believed.

Context: The Good News goes to Asia

Calvinist View: Unconditional election; "all who were appointed."

"And this place teacheth that faith dependeth on God's election." –John Calvin, *Calvin's Commentaries on the Bible*

"And this place teacheth that faith dependeth on God's election." –John Calvin, *Commentaries on the Bible*

Arminian Response: This passage is best translated in the middle-passive voice– "As many as set themselves to eternal life believed."

Comment: This so called "smoking gun" for predestation is not indeed such a proof text. The Greek word for "appointed," is Tasso and is not used elsewhere for ordination of salvation. This text shows an activation of purpose, not a decreeing of persons.

Quick Points:

1) Salvation was appointed for the human race.

2) Those who believe are activation, through grace, that which they have been called to.

From the Experts:

"He (Luke) is not speaking of what has been done from eternity, but what was then done, through the preaching of the Gospel. The original word (appointed) is not used once in Scripture to express eternal predestination of any kind." –John Wesley, *Explanatory Notes on the NT*

"It refers not to an eternal decree, but that then there was such an influence as to dispose them, or incline them, to lay hold on salvation." –Albert Barnes, *Notes on the New Testament Explanatory and Practical.*

The Bottom line: "This was a present operation of Divine grace working faith in the hearers." – John Wesley, *Explanatory Notes on the NT*

> **Notes:**

Acts 14:21-22 (NIV)
[21] They preached the good news in that city and won a large number of disciples. Then they returned to Lystra, Iconium and Antioch,
[22] strengthening the disciples and encouraging them to remain true to the faith. "We must go through many hardships to enter the kingdom of God," they said.

Context: Work in Derbe, Return to Antioch

Calvinist View: Believers needed encouraging, but the elect would remain true.

Arminian Response: Believers needed encouraging, to continue in the faith and not fall back.

Comment: It was not popular to be a Christian in the day of Acts 14. Persecution was growing, and actually aided in the missionary thrust.

Believers needed to be encouraged to not give up and return to Judaism or plain give up altogether.

Quick Points:

1) All disciples need encouraging.

2) There would not be a challenge to remain true, unless there was a danger of not doing so.

From the Experts:

"The truth was, that these were young converts; that they were surrounded by enemies, exposed to temptations and to dangers; that they had as yet but a slight acquaintance with the truths of the gospel, and that it was therefore important that they should be further instructed in the truth, and established in the faith of the gospel." –Albert Barnes, *Notes on the New Testament Explanatory and Practical.*

The Bottom line: The believers were encouraged to remain true in the face of opposition.

Notes:

Acts 16:14 (NIV)
[14] One of those listening was a woman named Lydia, a dealer in purple cloth from the city of Thyatira, who was a worshiper of God. The Lord opened her heart to respond to Paul's message".

Context: The Good News goes to Europe

Calvinist View: The Lord's opening of her heart shows predestination and election.

"Now, if the cause be demanded why the Lord opened one woman's heart alone, we must return unto that principle, that so many believe as we are ordained − to life." –John Calvin, *Commentaries on the Bible*

Arminian Response: Divine grace opened her heart, working through freewill.

Comment: Lydia was already responding to prevenient grace (Rom. 5:8), and this is a further working of God in relation to her obedient response to grace. God did not open her heart, without a response from Lydia to His grace.

Quick Points:

1) No one approaches God without the enabling and drawing of divine grace.

2) God had previously been at work on her heart and she had already responded.

3) Now her heart was ready to respond to Paul's message, which was a link to her ongoing experience of God.

From the Experts:

"…it is noteworthy that Lydia was already a worshipper of God." – I. Howard Marshall, *Kept by the Power of God*

"Some people are honest and yield to the Lord to open their hearts and others refuse all offers of God's dealings and are hardened." –*The Dake Annotated Reference Bible*

The Bottom line: Lydia's heart had been previously opened by God's drawing grace, and she responded freely.

Notes:

Acts 18:10 (NIV)

[10] For I am with you, and no one is going to attack and harm you, because I have many people in this city."

Context: Paul's vision from the Lord that assured success in the city.

Calvinist View: These were the elect (by decree) gathered for God's purpose.

Arminian Response: Many had responded to God's grace and were numbered with the believers.

Comment: Many had believed by faith as God's grace gathered them. Grace attracts and multiplies believers.

Quick Points:

1) Grace had gathered many hearts for the Kingdom.

2) They freely responded to this moving of grace.

3) God knew that this would happen and to whom.

From the Experts:

"Divine foreknowledge of the situation is thus indicated, but it is going too far to find in the verse the predestination of individuals to salvation." – I. Howard Marshall, *Kept by the Power of God*

"An encouragement for every Christian witness." –*The Wesley Bible*

The Bottom line: Grace naturally attracts the masses to believe.

Notes:

Acts 18:27 (NIV)

[27] When Apollos wanted to go to Achaia, the brothers encouraged him and wrote to the disciples there to welcome him. On arriving, he was a great help to those who by grace had believed.

Context: Apollos at Ephesus

Calvinist View: They believed because it was appointed for them to believe by grace.

"For the meaning thereof shall be this, that the faithful were illuminate by the grace of God, that they might believe;" –John Calvin, *Commentaries on the Bible*

Arminian Response: They believed because grace drew open hearts to a crisis moment of salvation.

Comment: Grace leads us to faith and into salvation. It is by grace that we are equipped and allowed by choice to believe, but not made to believe.

Quick Points:

1) Grace prepared them.

2) By faith they believed.

From the Experts:

"Faith in God is due to the grace of God." – I. Howard Marshall, *Kept by the Power of God*

"It is only by the grace of God that any man can believe and respond affirmatively to His call. But to assume that God wills that only a few shall believe and heed His call is to reject the testimony of 1 Timothy 2:4 that God wills all men shall come to the knowledge of the truth and be saved, and the testimony of Titus 2:11 that "the grace of God appeared for the salvation of all men" (RSV), and the testimony of many other categorical assertions in the Holy Scriptures." –Robert Shank, *Elect in the Son*

The Bottom line: Belief in Christ is preceded by and held by grace.

Notes:

Acts 26:19 (NIV)

[19] "So then, King Agrippa, I was not disobedient to the vision from heaven.

Context: Was it impossible for Paul to have disobeyed?

Calvinist View: Paul's argument is figurative language to highlight his obedience. Any disobedience would not have resulted in loss of salvation, but loss of fellowship.

Arminian Response: Paul exercised obedience in freewill to honor God.

Comment: Paul had a dramatic conversion experience that transformed his life from works oriented to grace. When an individual is so touched by Heaven, they soul has nothing on their mind, but doing the will of Heaven, but this does not preclude the possibility of not doing it. Paul was an instrument of freewill in action, not a robot living a decree out.

Quick Points:

1) Scripture does not use useless language to drive home points.

2) Paul was highlighting his obedience here.

3) His obedience was due to freewill, not due to inability to be disobedient.

From the Experts:

"Does this mean that he was free to have chosen to act otherwise? Could he have refused the divine offer of salvation? "…while the initiative of God in salvation is strongly stressed in Acts Luke does not teach that individuals are predestined to salvation so that a secret divine plan is fulfilled in their acceptance or rejection of the Gospel." – I. Howard Marshall, *Kept by the Power of God*

The Bottom line: Paul does not offer an empty argument (the possibility of his disobedience), but uses his obedience in freewill to honor Heaven (God).

> **Notes:**

Romans 3:10-18 (NIV)

[10] As it is written: "There is no one righteous, not even one;

[11] there is no one who understands, no one who seeks God.

[12] All have turned away, they have together become worthless; there is no one who does good, not even one."

[13] "Their throats are open graves; their tongues practice deceit." "The poison of vipers is on their lips."

[14] "Their mouths are full of cursing and bitterness."

[15] "Their feet are swift to shed blood;

[16] ruin and misery mark their ways,

[17] and the way of peace they do not know."

[18] "There is no fear of God before their eyes."

Context: Speed bumps to Righteousness

Calvinist View: All humans remain carnal even after all of God's gracious work. God sets up shop, covering such decadence but not removing it.

Arminian Response: Apart from God's grace none are righteous. Grace enables the worst sinner to heed salvations call and invitation. The old decadent heart can be made pure and a new heart through the Spirit.

Comment: No one is righteous before God apart from his help. No one. Grace restores the way to God, and makes a path for God to renew and restore that which was lost by the Fall (Gen. 3). To become holy, as God is holy, is through the purifying power of His grace. This is not a covering up, but burning up by the pure fire of the Spirit.

Quick Points:

1) No one is good enough for God left as they are.

2) Grace is the bridge for the fallen to interact with The Holy (God).

From the Experts:

"No responsible evangelical advocates total depravity in the *intensive sense* (that man is totally evil) only in the *extensive sense*: that the corruption of sin extends to the whole of man's being." –*Beacon Dictionary of Theology*

"Paul therefore rightly cites David and Isaiah, though they spoke primarily of their own age, and expressed what manner of men God sees, when he "looks down from heaven;" not what he makes them by his grace." John Wesley, *Explanatory Notes upon the New Testament*.

The Bottom line: No one pleases God when left to themselves.

Notes:

Romans 6:23 (NIV)

[23] For the wages of sin is death, but the gift of God is eternal life in Christ Jesus our Lord.

Context: Freedom from sin's bondage

Calvinist View: "If I must know whether or not I am saved by the state of my own faithfulness, it [salvation] is no gift at all." R.T. Kendall (Quote provided by Terry Chapman)

Arminian Response: "Eternal life...is a gift from God, which Scripture specifically declares must be received by faith." "By its very nature a gift must be willingly received." –Dave Hunt, *Debating Calvinism*

Comment: The wage of sin is death to whoever commits it– believer or non-believer (Ezek. 18:4, 20). For the believer, past sins are covered; future sins are eligible for forgiveness upon repentance.

Quick Points:

1) Sin leads to spiritual death.

2) Jesus' death paid for sin.

3) Unconfessed sin is harmful and can lead to spiritual death.

From the Experts:

"That man can accept or reject the "gift of...eternal life" (Romans 6:23) is required by the very nature of a gift and the fact that to be saved one must believe in the heart (Acts 8:37; Romans 10:9)." –Dave hunt, *Debating Calvinism*

"But the gift of God. Not the wages of man; not that which is due to him; but the mere gift and mercy of God. The apostle is careful to distinguish, and to specify that this is not what man deserves, but that which is gratuitously conferred on him." –Albert Barnes, *Notes on the New Testament Explanatory and Practical.*

The Bottom line: Sin brings death forever; God's life given freely brings life forever.

> **Notes:**

Romans 8:5-9 (NIV)

[5] Those who live according to the sinful nature have their minds set on what that nature desires; but those who live in accordance with the Spirit have their minds set on what the Spirit desires.

[6] The mind of sinful man is death, but the mind controlled by the Spirit is life and peace;

[7] the sinful mind is hostile to God. It does not submit to God's law, nor can it do so.

[8] Those controlled by the sinful nature cannot please God.

[9] You, however, are controlled not by the sinful nature but by the Spirit, if the Spirit of God lives in you. And if anyone does not have the Spirit of Christ, he does not belong to Christ.

Context: Power Rooted in Righteousness

Calvinist View: The sin nature is ever present, but covered by Christ.

Arminian Response: The sin nature is to be cleansed and the nature made new.

Comment: Some see this passage as inability to respond to God, calling such a thought the traditions of men. This passage follows on the footsteps of Paul's themes of sin, salvation, and now sanctification. It is a description and defining of life in the flesh vs. Spirit. Those who yield to the sin nature do not please God, but they do so by freewill, not inability by decree.

Quick Points:

1) The sin nature and Holy Spirit do not mix or coincide.

2) The sin nature is always hostile to God and His Spirit, which show the need for its death.

From the Experts:

"**He is none of his** – He is not a member of Christ; not a Christian; not in a state of salvation. A plain, express declaration, which admits of no exception. He that hath ears to hear, let him hear!" –John Wesley, *Explanatory Notes upon the New Testament.*

"*Is none of his.* Is not a Christian. This is a test of piety that is easily applied; and this settles the question. If a man is not influenced by the meek, pure, and holy spirit of the Lord Jesus, if he is not conformed to his image, if his life does not resemble that of the Saviour, he is a stranger to religion. No test could be more easily applied, and none is more decisive. It matters not what else he may have. He may be loud in his professions, amiable in his temper, bold in his zeal, or active in promoting the interests of his own party or denomination in the church; but if he has not the temper of the Saviour, and does not manifest his spirit, it is as sounding brass or a tinkling cymbal. May all who read this honestly examine themselves; and may they have that which is the source of the purest felicity, the spirit and temper of the Lord Jesus."

–Albert Barnes, *Notes on the New Testament Explanatory and Practical.*

The Bottom line: The sinful nature is opposed to spiritual life in humanity and needs to be removed by the Spirit.

Notes:

Romans 8:13 (NIV)

[13] For if you live according to the sinful nature, you will die; but if by the Spirit you put to death the misdeeds of the body, you will live,

Context: The New Victory of Sanctification

Calvinist View:

"…this verse means they will die physically, a premature death, because they deny the will of God for their lives." – Elmer Towns, *Bible Answers for Almost All Your Questions*

Arminian Response: "If you live to indulge your carnal propensities, you will sink to eternal death" –Albert Barnes, *Notes on the New Testament Explanatory and Practical.*

Comment: The elect or "saints" mentioned in the New Testament did not live according to the sinful nature, but had it conquered by the Spirit. The war (Galatians 5) between flesh and Spirit was over and ongoing obedience was the new fight. Believers are not to be sin nature defined. Such are not filling out the name of "saint."

Quick Points:

1) The Spirit is to subdue and conquer the sin nature in believers.

2) To tolerate of fee the sin nature is not the way of the elect.

3) Such a path will lead one out of the category of elect.

From the Experts:

"If any habitually live according to corrupt lustings, they will certainly perish in their sins, whatever they profess." –Matthew Henry, *Matthew Henry Concise Bible Commentary.*

The Bottom line: Failure to let God's Spirit deal with the sin nature will end badly for the believer, possibly even eternally.

> **Notes:**

Romans 8:15 (NIV)

[15] For you did not receive a spirit that makes you a slave again to fear, but you received the Spirit of sonship. And by him we cry, *"Abba*, Father."

Context: The New Victory in the Spirit

Calvinist View: Reception to sonship via election.

Arminian Response: Reception by grace into standing in God's family.

Comment: The natural flow of one becoming a Christian comes to becoming a child of God. The receiving of this right is freely by grace, not by works, or imputed election.

Quick Points:

1) Becoming a child of God is by faith.

2) Anyone who believes receives this right.

From the Experts:

"The spirit of bondage here seems directly to mean, those operations of the Holy Spirit by which the soul, on its first conviction, feels itself in bondage to sin, to the world, to Satan, and obnoxious to the wrath of God. This, therefore, and the Spirit of adoption, are one and the same Spirit, only manifesting itself in various operations, according to the various circumstances of the persons." –John Wesley, *Explanatory Notes upon the New Testament.*

The Bottom line: God wants humans to be part of His family.

Notes:

Romans 8:28-36 (NIV)

[28] And we know that in all things God works for the good of those who love him, who have been called according to his purpose.

[29] For those God foreknew he also predestined to be conformed to the likeness of his Son, that he might be the firstborn among many brothers.

[30] And those he predestined, he also called; those he called, he also justified; those he justified, he also glorified.

[31] What, then, shall we say in response to this? If God is for us, who can be against us?

[32] He who did not spare his own Son, but gave him up for us all-how will he not also, along with him, graciously give us all things?

[33] Who will bring any charge against those whom God has chosen? It is God who justifies.

[34] Who is he that condemns? Christ Jesus, who died-more than that, who was raised to life-is at the right hand of God and is also interceding for us.

[35] Who shall separate us from the love of Christ? Shall trouble or hardship or persecution or famine or nakedness or danger or sword?

[36] As it is written: "For your sake we face death all day long; we are considered as sheep to be slaughtered."

Context: Power Rooted in Righteousness

Calvinist View: Those predestined are the elect, conformed by God to the likeness of the Son.

"Hence Paul teaches us, that those whom he had spoken of as loving God, had been previously chosen by him." –John Calvin, *Commentaries on the Bible* (v.35) "Their salvation, beginning to end, is assured. –James White, *Debating Calvinism*

Arminian Response: God foreknew who would believe and planned salvation for humans before the fact. The believer "in Christ" is secure.

Comment: God knew who would believe and offered salvation to the whole world. Salvation was predestined to be offered to mankind. Grace enabled it to be offered. It is kept safe in the believer, by remaining to its author– Christ.

Quick Points:

1) Salvation was planned to be offered to all.

2) Those who receive it freely and remain in it will prove their calling that ends ultimately in glorification in heaven.

3) The promises of protection were not to become a freestanding loophole to the commandments and warnings of Scripture, but comfort.

From the Experts:

"The translation is, "For whom he did foreknow, he also did predestinate." The objects of predestination are those whom He foreknew. Predestination does not involve a predetermined plan only but also includes the individuals for whom the plan is devised. The goal of predestination is expressed in the phrase, "to be conformed to the image of his Son." –*AMG's Complete Word Study Dictionaries – The Complete Word Study Dictionary – New Testament.*

"God has a purpose of salvation for men, in accordance with which He calls them by the Gospel, and the persons described in this verse (8:28) are those who have answered this call, as is plain from the fact that they now love God." –I. Howard Marshall, *Kept by the Power of God*

"(v.35) Not who shall keep Christ from loving us, but who or what shall keep us from loving Him? This is the true idea, for the things listed here might affect men, but not Christ. If we will not permit them to affect our love for Christ, then we are safe from all danger of backsliding." –*The Dake Annotated Reference Bible*

"Election relates not merely to individuals, but to the entire body, and, accordingly, to individuals as members of the body." (Hoffman) –Robert Shank, *Elect in the Son*

The Bottom line: God predestined salvation, knowing who would believe.

Notes:

Romans 8:38-39 (NIV)

[38] For I am convinced that neither death nor life, neither angels nor demons, neither the present nor the future, nor any powers, [39] neither height nor depth, nor anything else in all creation, will be able to separate us from the love of God that is in Christ Jesus our Lord.

Context: Power Rooted in Righteousness

Calvinist View: This passage is the eternal security of the believer.

"Here is the Christian, all weakness in himself, despised and trampled underfoot by the world, triumphing over all existing, and all possible, and even impossible evils and opposition, having only this as his stay and support– that the God who has loved him, will never cease to love, keep, and defend him." –John Calvin, *Calvin's Commentaries on the Bible*

"The contrast is the grandest that can be conceived. Here is the Christian, all weakness in himself, despised and trampled underfoot by the world, triumphing over all existing, and all possible, and even impossible evils and opposition, having only this as his stay and support — that the God who has loved him, will never cease to love, keep, and defend him; yea, were everything created, everything except God himself, leagued against him and attempting his ruin." –John Calvin, *Commentaries on the Bible*

Arminian Response: Paul's purpose is to show what cannot afflict of separate the believer, but it does not mention the believer separating themselves from God. This is a beautiful passage of security by faith, not security from faith.

Comment: God loves the sinner and saint. God's love is shed in mercy for the sinner saved by grace, and the saint that has turned to a life of sin. This passage is not a decree of unconditional security, but look at what security of a faithful saint looks like.

Quick Points:

1) Nothing sneaks in and separates the believer from God.

2) This passage though is not highlighting security apart from Christ.

From the Experts:

"Nothing can keep us <u>who belong to Christ</u> from receiving the benefits of God's love for us." –*The Wesley Study Bible*

"To separate us from the love of God in Christ – Which will surely save, protect, deliver us who believe in, and through, and from, them all." –John Wesley, *Explanatory Notes on the NT*

"The true followers of Christ can never be forsaken by him." –Adam Clarke, *A Commentary and Critical Notes*

"The promises here are to those "who walk not after the flesh, but after the Spirit…No one who lives in sin can claim to be led by the Son of God." –Purkiser, *Security– The False & The True*

"Paul omits one significant reference, theologians have been arguing from this silence for centuries. Paul does not mention humans themselves. If there is not "anything else in all creation" that can separate us from God's love (v.39), would it not seem logical that the believer, who is certainly part of the creation, would be included?" – Clarence l. Bence, *Romans– A Bible Commentary in the Wesleyan Tradition*

The Bottom line: Believers are secure as they live for and obey Christ. There is no security apart from Him.

```
┌─────────────────────────────────────────────┐
│  ╭──────────╮                                 │
│  │ Notes:   │                                 │
│  ╰──────────╯                                 │
│                                               │
│                                               │
│                                               │
│                                               │
│                                               │
└─────────────────────────────────────────────┘
```

Romans 9:5-6 (NIV)

[5] Theirs are the patriarchs, and from them is traced the human ancestry of Christ, who is God over all, forever praised! Amen.
[6] It is not as though God's word had failed. For not all who are descended from Israel are Israel.

Context: Israel's Position and Election

Calvinist View:

"The general election of the people of Israel is no hindrance, that God should not from them choose by his hidden counsel those whom he pleases." –John Calvin, *Commentaries on the Bible*

Arminian Response: God chose the Hebrew people to be established in the line leading to the Messiah, but all would not be faithful along the way.

Comment: Though many failed in the history of the nation of Israel, God's purpose was fulfilled ultimately in Christ.

Quick Points:

1) Not all of Israel believed and received.

2) But this did not stop Jesus from coming as Messiah, as God had established His lineage.

From the Experts:

"Paul is thinking here of the nation rather than of the complete total of individuals who comprise it." – I. Howard Marshall, *Kept by the Power of God*

"Not all Israel. Not all the descendants of Jacob have the true spirit of Israelites, or are Jews in the scriptural sense of the term. Romans 2:28,29."
–Albert Barnes, *Notes on the New Testament Explanatory and Practical.*

The Bottom line: God's Word and plan never fails, though people do.

Notes:

Romans 9:10-13 (NIV)

[10] Not only that, but Rebekah's children had one and the same father, our father Isaac.

[11] Yet, before the twins were born or had done anything good or bad- in order that God's purpose in election might stand:

[12] not by works but by him who calls- she was told, "The older will serve the younger."

[13] Just as it is written: "Jacob I loved, but Esau I hated."

Context: Israel receives God's spiritual promise

Calvinist View: This text shows the 2-fold nature of election, those chosen and those not.

"God is love" does *not* mean does not mean that "God has the same kind of love and level of love for all things, including for each and every single individual human being." –James White, *Debating Calvinism*

Arminian Response: This text shows God's spiritual promise and the path He chose to unveil it, through the most free agents.

Comment: Jacob and Esau are good pictures of the two different paths a person can take: God's plan or Man's. Esau chose to serve self and Jacob though no saint would respond to grace. Their choices and actions indicated their internal desires and passions that revealed the true state of their hearts (James 1:14). Esau was not however planned and made to be rebellious. Sin took him there. God both knew Esau's choices, and planned to utilize Jacob. All of this is within the realm of freewill.

Quick Points:

1) God chose the descendants of Jacob over Esau's.

2) The line of Messiah would come through him.

3) Esau proved himself unworthy to be used.

From the Experts:

"Paul teaches the fact of a special predestination or election of the people of Israel to salvation, but it is equally clear that this predestination by no means guarantees the salvation of every Israelite or even all who hear the Gospel and respond to it." – I. Howard Marshall, *Kept by the Power of God*

I have loved Jacob – With a peculiar love; that is, the Israelites, the posterity of Jacob. And I have, comparatively,

hated Esau – That is, the Edomites, the posterity of Esau. But observe,

1. This does not relate to the person of Jacob or Esau

2. Nor does it relate to the eternal state either of them or their posterity.

"Thus far the apostle has been proving his proposition, namely, that the exclusion of a great part of the seed of Abraham, yea, and of Isaac, from the special promises of God, was so far from being impossible, that, according to the scriptures themselves, it had actually happened. He now introduces and refutes an objection. Malachi 1:2, 3." –John Wesley, *Explanatory Notes upon the New Testament*

The Bottom line: "God did not choose the descendants of Esau as the nation through which the Savior would come." –*The Wesley Bible*

> **Notes:**

Romans 9:14-15 (NIV)

[14] What then shall we say? Is God unjust? Not at all!

[15] For he says to Moses, "I will have mercy on whom I have mercy, and I will have compassion on whom I have compassion."

Context: God's Faithful Past History with Israel

Calvinist View: God expresses His sovereign will by having mercy on whom He wills, and whom He will not.

"God *mercies* whom He wills and *hardens* whom He wills." –James White, *Debating Calvinism*

Arminian Response: God as Almighty can choose to interact with humans in any way He sees as fit, but acts fairly to all humans.

Comment: "That election is conditioned on faith is clearly affirmed in the Scriptures. Consider the following propositions:

-Romans 11:6 says in effect, not of works, but of grace.

-Romans 4:1-5 says, not of works, but of faith.

-The Bible nowhere says, not of faith, but by grace.

-Romans 4:16 says, by faith, so that by grace.

-Ephesians 2:8 says, "By grace, through faith" –Robert Shank, *Elect in the Son*

Quick Points:

1) God uses a combination of Sovereignty and freewill in regards to humans.

2) He accomplishes His purpose (judging Pharaoh and his gods), within freedom of will (Pharaoh was sinful and his sins warranted judgment).

3) God did not single Pharaoh out unjustly. Because Pharaoh was set against the Lord, the Lord broke him. If Pharaoh would have not been sinful, God would not have stood against him.

From the Experts:

"I will have mercy on whom I will have mercy – According to the terms I myself have fixed.

And I will have compassion on whom I will have compassion – Namely, on those only who submit to my terms, who accept of it in the way that I have appointed."

–John Wesley, *Explanatory Notes upon the New Testament.*

"There is ample evidence elsewhere in Paul's writings and in the whole of Scripture to suggest that God's choice for salvation is more inclusive than exclusive." – Clarence l. Bence, Romans– A Bible Commentary in the Wesleyan Tradition

The Bottom line: God is answereable to no one, but does not deviate from holy love, by rejecting some souls just so a plan pans out.

Notes:

Romans 9:16-18 (NIV)

[16] It does not, therefore, depend on man's desire or effort, but on God's mercy. [17] For the Scripture says to Pharaoh: "I raised you up for this very purpose, that I might display my power in you and that my name might be proclaimed in all the earth." [18] Therefore God has mercy on whom he wants to have mercy, and he hardens whom he wants to harden.

Context: God's Faithfulness/ Human (Jewish) Unfaithfulness

Calvinist View: Since it does not depend on man's desire or effort (v.16), it is unconditional election. God raises up some people to be used and then end in damnation.

"…when the passage is allowed to speak for itself, it speaks of unconditional election in plainest terms." –James White, *Debating Calvinism*

"That our mind may be satisfied with the difference which exists between the elect and the reprobate, and may not inquire for any cause higher than the divine will, his purpose was to convince us of this — that it seems good to God to illuminate some that they may be saved, and to blind others that they may perish…" –John Calvin, *Commentaries on the Bible*

Arminian Response: The big picture in Romans 9 is God's choice of nations and how he will use them. God uses wicked people to complete His purpose, but the wickedness is from personal evil desires not an unalterable setting placed on them by God.

Comment: God as God can decide to show His great mercy on His terms. Man does not move an inch apart from God's grace– absolutely. Pharaoh was hardened based on what was already at work in his heart. God gave him freewill, and he chose badly. God knew he would and hardened him. The point here is not determinism, but God working freely utilizing the wills he allows us to use. From start to finish it is a God-thing.

Quick Points:

1) Salvation is by faith through grace.

2) It is also by works that one's faith is shown true (James 2:26), and we were created to perform good deeds (Ephesians 2:10).

3) God will not single out people to be wicked, but wicked people to be judged.

From the Experts:

"God has the right to reject those who will not accept the blessings on his own terms." –John Wesley, *Explanatory Notes Upon the NT*

"Yet "him that willeth" indicates that man can will to receive God's mercy. "Of God that showeth mercy" simply means that God makes the rules, not that man cannot respond to the offer of mercy." –Dave Hunt, *Debating Calvinism*

"No man can either save himself, or force God to save him. This is all Romans 9:16 says, not that some are predestined to salvation and others to damnation." –Dave Hunt, *Debating Calvinism*

"Here we have an instance of a wicked king resisting God's will to the point of destruction. At many points in God's dealings with Pharaoh the king could have submitted and escaped judgment. But he was too stubborn to do so and therefore God could not do otherwise than punish him for his sins and resistance." –*The Dake Annotated Reference Bible*

The Bottom line: While humans fail, God is faithful and will make sure true believers succeed. God is also above human scrutiny, but works within Bibical framework: salvation for God-seekers and judgment for sinners.

Notes:

Romans 9:19-21 (NIV)

[19] One of you will say to me: "Then why does God still blame us? For who resists his will?"

[20] But who are you, O man, to talk back to God? "Shall what is formed say to him who formed it, 'Why did you make me like this?'"

[21] Does not the potter have the right to make out of the same lump of clay some pottery for noble purposes and some for common use?

Context: God's Faithfulness/ Human (Jewish) Unfaithfulness

Calvinist View: God's Sovereign Will is carried out on humans both positive (election) and negative (damnation).

Arminian Response: God is Almighty and uses and moves people, but not against who they are in freewill.

Comment: No human is able to resist God, apart from God-given freewill. No human has the right to tell God what to do or how to call the shots. No human has the right apart from being able to by God's hand, to resist Him. Resistance is an exercise of grace and mercy, not mere human will.

Quick Points:

1) Humans cannot act apart from God's allowing.

2) This does not mean they are not free, but that their freedom is within His sovereign hand.

From the Experts:

"Side by side with the stress on the divine initiative in election and salvation there is a warning to show awe in the sight of God lest anyone should be cut off for failing to continue in His kindness." – I. Howard Marshall, *Kept by the Power of God*

"Of course we dare not judge God. But at the same time, we must also have confidence that God is "of purer eyes than to behold evil, and canst not look on iniquity" (Habakkuk 1:13), and cannot be tempted by evil, neither tempteth he any man" (James 1:13). That being the case, we can be confident that God would not cause man to sin." –Dave Hunt, *Debating Calvinism*

The Bottom line: God instigated salvation and start to finish it is a God thing: freewill, free grace, free life.

> **Notes:**

Romans 9:22-23 (NIV)

[22] What if God, choosing to show his wrath and make his power known, bore with great patience the objects of his wrath-prepared for destruction? [23] What if he did this to make the riches of his glory known to the objects of his mercy, whom he prepared in advance for glory—

Context: God's Promise of Righteousness

Calvinist View: These are the elect who have been prepared in advance for glory. "objects of his wrath"–prepared for destruction" refers to predestination (v.23).

"There are vessels prepared for destruction, that is, given up and appointed to destruction: they are also vessels of wrath, that is, made and formed for this end, that they may be examples of God's vengeance and displeasure." –John Calvin, *Commentaries on the Bible*

Arminian Response: Salvation was prepared in advance for those who will believe. It is the wide spectrum of salvation, not narrow lens of selective election.

Comment: God is highlighted and praised when he upholds His righteousness and judges sinners, as well as when saves the righteous in His salvation. Both work within the real of freewill.

Quick Points:

1) God was very patient with those who ultimately received His wrath.

2) God would rather glory from souls seeking Him.

3) Ultimately He will be praised either by enabling righteous seekers, or upholding His righteousness against the ungodly.

From the Experts:

"God's purpose for our redemption and salvation goes back before creation (Eph. 1:4)." –*The Wesley Bible*

"Romans 9 must be understood in the light of Romans 9:30-11:36, in which Paul affirms that, instead of acting arbitrarily toward men (as He has a right to do as sovereign Creator), God is governed in His actions by His purpose of grace toward all men (Romans 11:32, Titus 2:11, etc.)." –Robert Shank, *Elect in the Son*

The Bottom line: Those who believe are of those prepared for salvation, and those who do not– for destruction in Hell.

Notes:

Romans 10:13 (NIV)
[13] for, "Everyone who calls on the name of the Lord will be saved."

Context: Salvation for Jew and Gentile in the Present

Calvinist View: Anyone may call, but only the elect will be saved.

"Salvation is available for all people and races." John MacArthur, *The John MacArthur Study Bible*

Arminian Response: "He offers salvation to both (Jews and Gentiles) and saves all who ask Him in faith." –*The Wesley Bible*

Comment: The Lord has set things up so that all who respond to Him may be saved (John 1:12). He does not enable some, and constrain others. He aids all. Loves all. And knowing all, He knows who will be faithful and who will depart.

Quick Points:

1) Salvation from God is all encompassing in scope.

2) The system is not elect/ non-elect before salvation, but upon believing or disagreeing.

From the Experts:

"The gift is available to all– that is, all who will respond to the call of God with a call of their own." Clarence L. Bence, *Romans, A Bible Commentary in the Wesleyan Tradition*

"Jesus is Lord of both Jews and Gentiles. He offers salvation to both and saves all who ask Him in faith. He is rich in that He is always ready to save those who call upon Him." *–The Wesley Bible*

The Bottom line: Salvation is offered by God through faith to all, but not accepted by all.

> **Notes:**

Romans 11:2 (NIV)
[2] God did not reject his people, whom he foreknew. Don't you know what the Scripture says in the passage about Elijah– how he appealed to God against Israel:

Context: Some of Israel Believes

Calvinist View: " I know not what, by which God foresees what sort of being any one will be, but that good pleasure, according to which he has chosen those as sons to himself, who, being not yet born, could not have procured for themselves his favor." –John Calvin, *Commentaries on the Bible*

Arminian Response: The focus here is Israel and God preserving salvation history, not individual election.

Comment: "Though the mass of the nation, therefore, should be cast off, yet it would not follow that God had violated any promise or compact; or that he had rejected *any* whom he had foreknown as his true people. God makes no covenant of salvation with those who are in their sins; and if the unbelieving and the wicked, however many external privileges they may have enjoyed, are rejected, it does not follow that he has been unfaithful to one whom he had foreknown or designated as an heir of salvation." –Albert Barnes, *Notes on the New Testament Explanatory and Practical.*

Quick Points:

1) This is preserving the line for salvation through the coming Messiah.

2) Those who were unfaithful and sinned, did not make the cut, no matter what title they gave themselves.

From the Experts:

"God's acceptance of those who accept His offer of free salvation." –*The Wesley Bible*

"The passages positing foreknowledge (1 Pet. 1:2; Rom. 8:28-30; 11:2) and predestination (Eph. 1:3-14; Rom. 8:28-30) obviously comprehend individuals, but only within the context of the corporate election of Israel." –Robert Shank, *Elect in the Son*

The Bottom line: God knows who is going to be saved, but lets salvation history freely play out.

> **Notes:**

Romans 11:28-32 (NIV)

[28] As far as the gospel is concerned, they are enemies on your account; but as far as election is concerned, they are loved on account of the patriarchs,

[29] for God's gifts and his call are irrevocable.

[30] Just as you who were at one time disobedient to God have now received mercy as a result of their disobedience,

[31] so they too have now become disobedient in order that they too may now receive mercy as a result of God's mercy to you.

[32] For God has bound all men over to disobedience so that he may have mercy on them all.

Context: The Salvation of Israel

Calvinist View:

"He has mentioned gifts and calling; which are to be understood, according to a figure in grammar, as meaning the gift of calling: and this is not to be taken for any sort of calling but of that, by which God had adopted the posterity of Abraham into covenant; since this is especially the subject here, as he has previously, by the word, election, designated the secret purpose of God, by which he had formerly made a distinction between the Jews and the Gentiles." –John Calvin, *Commentaries on the Bible*

Arminian Response:

"For though "the gifts of God are without repentance" yet one can reject the gifts of God, which he receives. The Lord knoweth His own, even if some believers do fall away from faith."– James Arminius, *Complete Works of Arminius.*

Comment: There were certain things, "gifts and call," that had to be set in place regardless of faith for the Messiah to bring salvation. This does not mean God hog-tied people to accomplish this. He accomplished it through faith.

Quick Points:

1) Nothing could alter God's set plan to bring salvation to the world.

2) Disobedience was dealt with.

3) God's end plan was to bring mercy.

From the Experts:

"There is no reason to suppose that election excludes the need for faith or that election automatically produces faith." – I. Howard Marshall, *Kept by the Power of God*

"(v. 32) is a refrain of his (Paul's) earlier statement that "all have sinned and fall short of the glory of God, and are justified freely by his grace" (3:23, 24)."

–Clarence l. Bence, Romans– *A Bible Commentary in the Wesleyan Tradition*

"irrevocable: Cannot be changed– God's plan for the salvation of both Jew and Gentile will be fulfilled." –*The Wesley Bible*

The Bottom line: God's plans and purpose are not hindered by unbelief, nor do they sidestep freewill.

Notes:

Romans 15:15 (NIV)

[15] I have written you quite boldly on some points, as if to remind you of them again, because of the grace God gave me

Context: Christian Service and Fellowship

Calvinist View: Grace given as a commodity in election.

Arminian Response: Paul received the grace that was given him freely.

Comment: God gave Paul grace to encourage the Roman believers, to not forget about ministering to the Gentiles. Grace comes freely from God and is not to be held in but passed on to others thought adopting the humbling servant attitude of Christ.

Quick Points:

1) God's grace was given to Paul for salvation and ministry.

2) Paul was going to encourage the Roman believers to follow his example in God's grace.

From the Experts:

He had written to remind them of their duties and their dangers, because God had appointed him the minister of Christ to the Gentiles. –Matthew Henry, *Matthew Henry Concise Bible Commentary*.

The Bottom line: Paul was given the grace and heart for the Gentiles.

> ### Notes:

1 Corinthians 1:30-31 (NIV)

[30] It is because of him that you are in Christ Jesus, who has become for us wisdom from God- that is, our righteousness, holiness and redemption. [31] Therefore, as it is written: "Let him who boasts boast in the Lord."

Context: Importance of Genuine Unity

Calvinist View: "It is because" of eternal decree and election of God, that humans are in Christ.

Arminian Response: "It is because" of God that we are able to come to Christ as God has planned out eternal salvation given by faith.

Comment: It is because of Jesus that we have all the spiritual benefits we have as Christians. Christ not only brings these things to us, but "is" these things in us (righteousness, etc.). The believer does not just had the appearance of the qualities of God, but has the real deal with God in us.

Quick Points:

1) Christ is the source of the believer's spiritual life.

2) He blesses the believer with these qualities throughout their person, as Christ is in them.

3) It is not merely a covering over of these qualities.

From the Experts:

"Even the good which you possess is granted by God, for it is by and through him that Christ Jesus comes, and all the blessings of the Gospel dispensation." –Adam Clarke, *A Commentary and Critical Notes*

"Out of his free grace and mercy. Are ye engrafted into Christ Jesus, who is made unto us that believe wisdom, who were before utterly foolish and ignorant." –John Wesley, *Explanatory Notes upon the New Testament*

"By the medium, or through the work of Christ, this mercy has been conferred on you." –Albert Barnes, *Notes on the New Testament Explanatory and Practical.*

The Bottom line: All that we are as Christians is from being "in" Christ, and Christ in us.

Notes:

1 Corinthians 2:14 (NIV)

[14] The man without the Spirit does not accept the things that come from the Spirit of God, for they are foolishness to him, and he cannot understand them, because they are spiritually discerned.

Context: Importance of Genuine Unity

Calvinist View: This text shows the utter depravity of man, who cannot reach out to grace but must have it thrust upon him.

Arminian Response: This text shows the dead end of human depravity, and the need for God's grace to reach out before a person is ready to be saved, so they may respond by faith.

Comment: Without the Spirit at work in the heart, there is no spiritual understanding. God by His grace lifts the spiritual veil (2 Cor. 4:3) and quickens the spiritual nature by grace.

Quick Points:

1) Humans do not seek God without his help.

2) Grace allows God's Spirit to work with us.

3) Grace is the link to human freedom created by God.

From the Experts:

"Paul is referring not to the Gospel but to the "deep things of God" (1 Cor. 2:10), which Peter says "the unlearned and unstable" twist to their own destruction (2 Peter 3:16). –Dave Hunt, *Debating Calvinism*

The Bottom line: Again, this is not inability based on a decree of God, but inability due to sin nature. If you are not spiritually alive everything is "clear as mud."

Notes:

1 Corinthians 3:16-17 (NIV)
[16] Don't you know that you yourselves are God's temple and that God's Spirit lives in you?
[17] If anyone destroys God's temple, God will destroy him; for God's temple is sacred, and you are that temple.

Context: Humans as God's Temple

Calvinist View: Destruction of rewards or blessings but not loss of eternal life.

Arminian Response: Destroying God's temple suggests disobedience, so the destruction of the individual is in the form of loss of eternal life (if sin is left outstanding).

Comment: Rebellion in the form of desecration of human bodies receives not just a slap on the wrist, but judgment for sin. Such sin left unrepented of will result in eternal separation from God (which would be the result of a life of sin).

Quick Points:

1) God will destroy the sinner.

2) A sinner is a state of being– Sinner's sin.

3) If you sin you are a sinner, and unrepentant believers sinning will be destroyed.

From the Experts:

"He shall not be saved at all." –John Wesley, *Explanatory Notes Upon the NT*

The Bottom line: Our bodies are to honor God, not dishonor, which would be sin.

Notes:

1 Corinthians 5:5 (NIV)
[5] hand this man over to Satan, so that the sinful nature may be destroyed and his spirit saved on the day of the Lord.

Context: Immorality in the Church

Calvinist View: It does not mean to deprive him of salvation, since it is not the church that grants salvation to begin with. When a Christian is in fellowship with the Lord and with the local church, he enjoys a special protection from Satan. But when he is out of fellowship with God and excommunicated from the local church, he is "fair game" for the enemy. God could permit Satan to attack the offender's body so that the sinning believer would repent and return to the Lord. –Warren Weirsbe, *Bible Exposition Commentary (BE Series) – New Testament – The Bible Exposition Commentary – New Testament, Volume 1.*

Arminian Response:

"**Of the flesh** – Unless prevented by speedy repentance." –John Wesley, *Explanatory Notes upon the New Testament.*

Comment: Some have taken this action to mean excommunication from the church, while others disagree. This action of giving a sinning Christian over to Satan was to be remedial. It was to bring torment on the individual to draw them back to the Cross. If they died before their repentance was complete, they would not be in Heaven.

Quick Points:

1) The point of this exercise was to pronounce judgment on sin, with the possibility of restoration.

2) This was not a believer who would be cast out of the fellowship and still be allowed into Heaven without a change of heart.

From the Experts:

"But the soul found mercy at the hand of God; for such a most extraordinary interference of God's power and justice, and of Satan's influence, could not fail to bring the person to a state of the deepest humiliation and contrition; and thus, while the flesh was destroyed, the spirit was saved in the day of the Lord Jesus." -Adam Clarke, *A Commentary and Critical Notes.*

The Bottom line: This was a tough exercise to judge sin and try to restore a sinner.

```
Notes:



```

1 Corinthians 9:27 (NIV)

[27] No, I beat my body and make it my slave so that after I have preached to others, I myself will not be disqualified for the prize.

Context: The Church and workers

Calvinist View: This is a disqualification of rewards, not of salvation. It may also be a serious warning used to keep people in line, though not a possible reality.

Arminian Response: The great Apostle warns of the possibility of missing out on [salvation], if he lived different than he preached.

Comment: Paul did not live in fear of losing his salvation, but he knew where an undisciplined spiritual life could lead even him– away from Christ.

Quick Points:

1) Paul is issuing an actual warning here.

2) He encouraged discipline to reign in his life.

3) The "prize" was not just rewards, but the ultimate prize of eternal life.

From the Experts:

"It is evident then, that one who has experienced the blessing of holiness, can lose it. He need not; he should not– but still he may. There is a possibility he may fall away." –Bishop B.T. Roberts, *Holiness Teachings*

Disqualified: "reprobate, rejected, castaway. It does not mean a "cracked pot," fit to keep, as some teach, but to become Christless and literally rejected." –*The Dake Annotated Reference Bible*

"St. Paul was certainly an elect person...and yet he declares it was possible he himself might become disqualified. (Wesley)" –*The Wesley Bible*

The Bottom line: The Bible contains real, not placebo, warnings.

> **Notes:**

2 Corinthians 5:21 (NIV)
[21] God made him who had no sin to be sin for us, so that in him we might become the righteousness of God.

Context: Christian Ministry

Calvinist View: This righteousness is imputed, since the heart is still depraved.

Arminian Response: This righteousness is imparted, as the heart has been cleansed. It is covered by the Blood, which has cleansed the individual from all sin (1 Jn. 1:9).

Comment: Scripture says "in Him" we might become the righteousness of God. This means the actual righteousness brought into our being by Christ. Not brought near and not affecting, but messed in union with Christ in purity.

Quick Points:

1) Becoming righteous is by the power of God.

2) This is "in Christ."

3) This is not a building over a depraved "sink-hole", but a state of change from sinful to righteous, by removal, not stacking.
From the Experts:

"In His death He took the punishment for our sin so that we might be forgiven and the righteousness of God might become a reality in our lives."
—*The Wesley Bible*

The Bottom line: Entering into and remaining in union with Christ provides God's righteousness for the saint.

Notes:

2 Corinthians 6:1 (NIV)
[1] As God's fellow workers we urge you not to receive God's grace in vain.

Context: Paul's Suffering in Ministry

Calvinist View: Since believers are elect and cannot become unelected, the warning in this verse can only mean losing fellowship and closeness, but not eternal position and life.

Arminian Response: Paul warns about treating God's grace lightly and losing out. This is a total loss of eternal life. It may start with an indifferent attitude or action, but ends in eternal loss.

Comment: "In vain" means the same today as it did in Paul's day– failing to have the desired result. This verse speaks of receiving God's grace in a manner that results in failure. Failure meaning total failure. Not partial failure, or missing some points of reward, but missing out entirely. Take it at face value.

Quick Points:

1) The Bible does not use empty warnings.

2) If it were a warning with limits (temporal, rewards, etc.) Paul would have differentiated.

3) "In vain" means utter loss.

From the Experts:

"If this is a correct interpretation (the appeal for believers to follow their initial act of faith), then the possibility exists that Christians may receive God's grace to no purpose after conversion and so become backsliders." (Explanation added) – I. Howard Marshall, *Kept by the Power of God*

The "grace of God" here means evidently the gracious offer of reconciliation and pardon. And the sense is, "We entreat you not to neglect or slight this offer of pardon, so as to lose the benefit of it, and be lost. It is offered freely and fully. It may be partaken of by all, and all may be saved. But it may also be slighted, and all the benefits of it will then be lost." –Albert Barnes, *Notes on the New Testament Explanatory and Practical.*

The Bottom line: It is possible to treat God's offering of salvation wrongly and miss out, at any stop on the Christian journey. This does not need to be the case though.

Notes:

Galatians 1:15-16 (NIV)

[15] But when God, who set me apart from birth and called me by his grace, was pleased
[16] to reveal his Son in me so that I might preach him among the Gentiles, I did not consult any man,

Context: Concern for True Gospel

Calvinist View: The irresistible call of Paul by God's grace paid no attention to Paul's freewill.

"God's grace paid no heed to Paul's "freewill;" it overwhelmed him, changed him, resurrected him, and gave him a new heart– without Paul's assistance."
–John Calvin, *Calvin's Commentaries on the Bible*

Arminian Response: God called Paul based on Paul's place in the bigger spectrum of His plan, and on who Paul would naturally be with freewill responding to the Divine Will.

Comment: God wanted Paul to be the Apostle Paul, not Ruffus, or Tacitus. He had a preordained position he wanted filled by Paul, and Paul filled it by responding obediently, but freely, and God's will was fulfilled.

Quick Points:

1) Paul had a unique calling to spread the Gospel that was unique to him.

2) This calling was to service and salvation, unique and yet part of the universal plan of free salvation and service.

From the Experts:

Set me apart for an apostle, as he did Jeremiah for a prophet. Jeremiah 1:5. Such an unconditional predestination as this may consist, both with God's justice and mercy.– John Wesley, *Explanatory Notes upon the New Testament.*

The meaning is, that God had in his secret purposes set him apart to be an apostle. It does not mean that he had actually called him in his infancy to the work, for this was not so, but that he designed him to be an important instrument in his hands in spreading the true religion. –Albert Barnes, *Notes on the New Testament Explanatory and Practical.*

The Bottom line: God gave Paul a special asignment from birth, but did not roll over his frewill in the process.

Notes:

Galatians 5:19-21 (NIV)

[19] The acts of the sinful nature are obvious: sexual immorality, impurity and debauchery;

[20] idolatry and witchcraft; hatred, discord, jealousy, fits of rage, selfish ambition, dissensions, factions

[21] and envy; drunkenness, orgies, and the like. I warn you, as I did before, that those who live like this will not inherit the kingdom of God.

Context: Works of the flesh

Calvinist View: These are sins that have been forgiven of the elect saint.

[v.21- inherit] "…signifies to possess by hereditary right; for by no right but that of adoption, as we have seen in other passages, do we obtain eternal life." –John Calvin, *Calvin's Commentaries on the Bible*

Arminian Response: These are sins that the "saints" of God do not exhibit, nor practice.

Comment: It is a perplexing dilemma that one comes to when a belief (Calvinism) says that saved people can reflect the works of the flesh and yet make it into the kingdom of God, when Paul writes that they "will not inherit the kingdom of God." Who is right? Paul, the Apostle speaking by Divine inspiration, or John Calvin?

Quick Points:

1) The issue is the action of doing the sin, not whether you are a Christian or not.

2) Christ did not die for sin, for us to reign in sin.

3) Will not inherit: Christian or non-Christian who practices these.
From the Experts:

"Shall not inherit—They are not children of God, and therefore cannot inherit the kingdom which belongs only to the children of the Divine family." –Adam Clarke., *A Commentary and Critical Notes*

"No man who commits these sins will inherit the kingdom of God unless he confesses and puts them out of his life (v.21, 1 Cor. 6:9-11). Let any man claim that he can be saved and yet live in these sins and judgment will decide whether he or Paul is right." –*The Dake Annotated Reference Bible*

The Bottom line: Just as works prove ones faith, such workings of the flesh ultimately can deny one's faith.

Notes:

The Problem with Calvinist Predestination.

Ephesians 1:3-5 (NIV)
[3] Praise be to the God and Father of our Lord Jesus Christ, who has blessed us in the heavenly realms with every spiritual blessing in Christ.
[4] For he chose us in him before the creation of the world to be holy and blameless in his sight. In love
[5] he predestined us to be adopted as his sons through Jesus Christ, in accordance with his pleasure and will-

Context: Mighty Blessings in Christ

Calvinist View: God decided beforehand who would be saved, in His Sovereignty.

"And since the same Apostle elsewhere declares that the grace which is now manifested by the Gospel "was given us in Christ Jesus before the world began," (2 Tim 1:9), I am resolved to adhere to it firmly even to the end." –John Calvin, *Institutes of the Christian Religion.*

Arminian Response: The Believer identifies in Christ's chosen status (Isa. 42:1), through salvation in Christ. Election and predestination work with foreknowledge.

"Predestination precedes persons, in respect to their actual existence, not as they are considered by the Deity. It refers to causes, before they actually exist, but not before they are foreseen by God from eternity, though, in the foresight of God, they exist, not as the causes of predestination, but as a condition requisite in the object." James Arminius, *Complete Works of Arminius*.

Comment: (see From the Experts)

Quick Points:

1) God's choosing of believers is for salvation (in general).

2) God planned the process long ago for those who would believe.

3) This is not separating election, but category by activation. Activation of the calling.

From the Experts:

"Salvation is divinely initiated…the human will is awakened by prevenient grace and the continuing ministry of the Holy Spirit, must cooperate with divine grace and receive by faith the gift of God. God has sovereignly predestinated the conditions upon which He will save us eternally. The power to believe is of God; the act of believing necessarily belongs to man." –*Beacon Dictionary of Theology*

"Having predestinated us to the adoption of sons – Having foreordained that all who afterwards believed should enjoy the dignity of being sons of God, and joint heirs with Christ. **According to the good pleasure of his will** – According to his free, fixed, unalterable purpose to confer this blessing on all those who should believe in Christ, and those only." –John Wesley, *Explanatory Notes on the NT*

"(Predestined) Here it is presented not as a capricious, arbitrary or whimsical exercise of raw will or unreasoned impulse, but as the expression of a deliberate and wise plan which purposes to redeem those undeserving sinners whom God freely favors as the objects of His mercy. Because it is neither possible nor permissible for us to pry into God's secret counsel, it is not proper to be fixated with determining who the predestined are. Instead, we should contemplate the glories of what they are predestined to, i.e., salvation, adoption, or glory."–*AMG's Complete Word Study Dictionaries – The Complete Word Study Dictionary – New Testament*.

–"Predestined "

"Either persons or the plan of salvation–

Problems with deterministic (some saved, some damned) view of predestination–

1. Takes emphasis away from God's love "A rewriting of John 3:16 "God so loved the predestined world [not "the world"], that He gave His only begotten Son."

2. Justice– Damning people to Hell before committed personal sins?

3. Contradicts what we know of God's will for all men. Ezek. 18:3, 32; 2 Pet. 3:9

"Our freedom– our freewill– to embrace or reject the gracious provisions of our salvation is a God-given ability. We are totally dependent on God as He works His great salvation in and through us; but we are allowed to accept or reject this grace." –Mark A. Holmes, Ephesians, *a Bible Commentary in the Wesleyan Tradition.*

"Chosen to be holy and without blame" (Ephesians 1:4) describes not salvation but a special blessing for the saved." –Dave Hunt, *Debating Calvinism*

"Paul testifies indeed that we were chosen before the foundation of the world; but, he adds, in Christ (Eph. 1:4)." –Robert Shank, *Elect in the Son*

The Bottom line: God has previously planned out salvation, but this does not limit the scope of those who may believe.

Notes:

Ephesians 1:13 (NIV)

¹³ And you also were included in Christ when you heard the word of truth, the gospel of your salvation. Having believed, you were marked in him with a seal, the promised Holy Spirit,

Context: Mighty Blessings in Christ

Calvinist View: Being marked and sealed is linked to eternal predestination in election. The one who believes has already been marked and sealed.

Arminian Response: "Having believed" the rest follows…marked and sealed, not before. Faith shows election to salvation.

Comment: Scripture becomes something it was never intended to, when you read into notions never intended. The hearer was included with Christ when heard the word, and having believed comes sealing and marking. Notice the flow and order. Marked and sealed after believing, not believing because a decree in eternity past sealed and marked.

Quick Points:

1) The believers spoken of were included in Christ, after they heard the Truth.

2) Follow the flow: they believed, then were sealed, not reverse or before.

From the Experts:

"Holy both in his nature and in his operations, and promised to all the children of God. The sealing seems to imply,

1. A full impression of the image of God on their souls.

2. A full assurance of receiving all the promises, whether relating to time or eternity. –John Wesley, *Explanatory Notes on the NT*

"He seals, that is, signifies God's ownership and protection of those who belong to Him." –*Beacon Dictionary of Theology*

"All that we are told is that God foreordains those who believe to become holy and to be his sons." [1:3-14] –I. Howard Marshall, *Kept by the Power of God*

'The Holy Spirit in our lives is God's seal or mark of ownership." –*The Wesley Bible*

The Bottom line: Those marked by the Spirit…first believed.

> **Notes:**

Ephesians 1:12-14 (NIV)

[12] in order that we, who were the first to hope in Christ, might be for the praise of his glory.

[13] And you also were included in Christ when you heard the word of truth, the gospel of your salvation. Having believed, you were marked in him with a seal, the promised Holy Spirit,

[14] who is a deposit guaranteeing our inheritance until the redemption of those who are God's possession- to the praise of his glory.

Context: Mighty Blessings in Christ

Calvinist View: Their inheritance was guaranteed because they were elect.

Arminian Response: The guarantee was rooted and held with the words "having believed," which was to be continued experience.

Comment: The seal of the Holy Spirit is the result of believing. It is not based on a decree for certain individuals, other than those who believe. It is also a protective measure for those who have believed and are believing. It is not an object that can be separated from the presence and person of Christ and His Spirit. Faith and belief keep this blessing a current protective and relational measure,

Quick Points:

1) To be sealed is not irrevocable.

2) Sealing occurred by believing– why would one expect it to continue with faith ceasing?

From the Experts:

"All that we are told is that God foreordains those who believe to become holy and to be His sons. –I. Howard Marshall, *Kept by the Power of God*

"The sealing was the result of believing, and that was the result of hearing the gospel." –Albert Barnes, *Notes on the New Testament Explanatory and Practical.*

The Bottom line: Sealing is like a "check mark" of approval on Christians who have the Spirit by faith, and live out the description of a Christian.

Notes:

Ephesians 2:1-2 (NIV)
[1] As for you, you were dead in your transgressions and sins,
[2] in which you used to live when you followed the ways of this world and of the ruler of the kingdom of the air, the spirit who is now at work in those who are disobedient.

Context: Mighty Blessings in Christ

Calvinist View: Dead denotes incapable of responding to God, so God had to activate salvation decreed from before time, for the elect so they can respond and believe.

Arminian Response: Dead denotes a state of being without Christ. Grace beckons and allows the sinner to respond by faith to Christ.

Comment: Does this refer to God sovereignly saving those He has predestined so they can believe?

Quick Points:

1) Everyone starts out separated from God by nature.

2) God's grace reaches out to such a state.

3) Grace goes before salvation by faith.

From the Experts:

"The point of Paul's argument is that men in such a state that they cannot save themselves by works, but when God calls them by the Gospel they can make the response by faith." –I. Howard Marshall, *Kept by the Power of God*

The Bottom line: Grace enables the sinner to respond and be saved.

> **Notes:**

Ephesians 2:7-9 (NIV)
[7] in order that in the coming ages he might show the incomparable riches of his grace, expressed in his kindness to us in Christ Jesus. [8] For it is by grace you have been saved, through faith- and this not from yourselves, it is the gift of God- [9] not by works, so that no one can boast.

Context: Mighty Blessings in Christ

Calvinist View: This grace is for the elect alone. "Paul says not that the beginning of salvation is of grace, but "by grace are ye saved," "not of works, lest any man should boast," (Eph 2:8, 9). – John Calvin, *Institutes of the Christian Religion*.

Arminian Response: Grace is universal in scope and capability, but narrow by the few who make use of it.

Comment: Good works prove and flow out from an active believer (2:10), but do not gain merit or help Christ's sacrifice along. Grace and faith are active in the hearts of all who believe.

Quick Points:

1) Grace is given by God so people can believe freely.

2) Faith is a response to God's grace, not a mechanical outpouring of decreed salvation.

From the Experts:

"Without the grace or power to believe no man ever did or can believe; but with that power the act of faith is a man's own. God never believes for any man, no more than he repents for him: the penitent, through this grace enabling him, believes for himself: nor does he believe necessarily, or impulsively when he has that power; the power to believe may be present long before it is exercised, else, why the solemn warnings with which we meet every where in the word of God, and threatenings against those who do not believe? Is not this a proof that such persons have the power but do not use it? They believe not, and therefore are not established. This, therefore, is the true state of the case: God gives the power, man uses the power thus given, and brings glory to God: without the power no man can believe; with it, any man may. –Adam Clarke, *A Commentary and Critical Notes*.

"Paul injects "by faith" while he is talking about salvation "by grace." The word "gift" is referring back to grace not faith." –Rev. Terry Chapman

The Bottom line: Faith is the way to respond to and please God.

Notes:

Ephesians 5:5-7 (NIV)

[5] For of this you can be sure: No immoral, impure or greedy person- such a man is an idolater- has any inheritance in the kingdom of Christ and of God.
[6] Let no one deceive you with empty words, for because of such things God's wrath comes on those who are disobedient.
[7] Therefore do not be partners with them.

Context: God's Power for Love and Work

Calvinist View: Since sins have been paid for "once for all" sin has no power over believers, so one of the Elect may have bad fruit, but be saved.

Arminian Response: What you do defines who you are, what you believe. The elect are not "disobedient" in an ongoing sense.

Comment: Actions define the heart work of God in a person. We are not saved but works, but deeds eventually give others a pretty good picture of where a person stands in life, in living belief. Anyone claiming to be a Christian and living like the Devil, denies themselves.

Quick Points:

1) Persons doing such actions (Christian or non-Christian) fall under such judgment.

2) Being a Christian is not a position above having to deal with the penalty of sins committed (through Christ). Salvation is not like a necklace to be worn, allowing the bearer impunity from the effects of sinning.

3) Salvation is to be from sin, not to sin.

From the Experts:

"There is no exception here for those who were once believers." –Purkiser, *Security– The False & The True*

"Suffer no man to persuade you that any of these things are innocent, or that they are unavoidable frailties of human nature; they are all sins and abominations in the sight of God; those who practice them are children of disobedience; and on account of such practices the wrath of God." –Adam Clarke, *A Commentary and Critical Notes.*

The Bottom line: God's children do not act like the Devil in cycles of life.

Notes:

Philippians 1:27 (NIV)

[27] Whatever happens, conduct yourselves in a manner worthy of the gospel of Christ. Then, whether I come and see you or only hear about you in my absence, I will know that you stand firm in one spirit, contending as one man for the faith of the gospel

Context: Difficult Circumstances Paul Faced

Calvinist View: These works are reflective of the elect, but are not essential for salvation that has been planned and decreed.

"…that they endure persecutions on his account, as though he had said that their adoption can no more be separated from the cross, than Christ can be torn asunder from himself." –John Calvin, *Calvin's Commentaries on the Bible*

Arminian Response: The Christian is to live worthy of the Gospel. God has set a standard for living that is to be heeded, and infringement of can result in hindrance of eternal destiny.

Comment: Paul's admonition is for the believers to live a godly life. What if they didn't? Would it matter? Would it cost more than loss of fellowship in this life? Possibly. All seeds of rebellion end somewhere, and ultimately if not checked by God will end in separation from God even for one who was once a believer.

Quick Points:

1) We need to always live worthy of the Gospel.

2) We need to be unified as the Body of Christ.

3) Such living will keep us secure in Christ, as we prove our faith (James 2:17).

From the Experts:

"For our citizenship is in heaven; but in this last verse he puts heaven in the place of the Church, and this is all right; for he, who is not a member of the Church of Christ on earth, can have no right to the kingdom of heaven, and he who does not walk worthy of the Gospel of Christ cannot be counted worthy to enter through the gates into the city of the eternal King." –Adam Clarke, *A Commentary and Critical Notes*.

The Bottom line: Conduct matters to go as we live out our salvation.

Notes:

Philippians 1:29 (NIV)

[29] For it has been granted to you on behalf of Christ not only to believe on him, but also to suffer for him,

Context: Paul's Difficulties

Calvinist View: Granted denotes a Sovereign decree by God.

Arminian Response: God grants believers the faith and grace they need and desire.

Comment: Faith is granted us by God's grace, and yet it is set up to work within the free human response to God.

Quick Points:

1) Faith is a tool given to us by God.

2) God has made it so you can believe, not that you must believe.

From the Experts:

"(Philippians 1:29) does not say that faith to believe is a gift without responsibility on man's part, but that the privilege to believe on Christ has been granted." –Dave Hunt, *Debating Calvinism*

The Bottom line: Faith has been entrusted to us to be used wisely, and choose God.

> **Notes:**

Philippians 2:22 (NIV)

[22] But you know that Timothy has proved himself, because as a son with his father he has served with me in the work of the gospel.

Context: Loving Exhortation to Humility and Unity

Calvinist View: Timothy had proved himself because he was an elect saint.

Arminian Response: Timothy proved he had faith and was of the Christian faith and ministry.

Comment: Young Timothy had proved himself with Paul and the other believers. His works/ deeds and life witness proved his faith.

Quick Points:

1) A godly example is important.

2) We need to be concerned with how godly our example can be, instead of what can I get by with and still be a Christian.

From the Experts:

"You have had evidence among yourselves how faithfully Timothy devoted himself to the promotion of the gospel, and how constantly he served with me. –Albert Barnes, *Notes on the New Testament Explanatory and Practical.*

The Bottom line: A good example proves our faith before others.

> **Notes:**

Philippians 3:18 (NLT)
[18] For I have told you often before, and I say it again with tears in my eyes, that there are many whose conduct shows they are really enemies of the cross of Christ.

Context: Paul's Example of Unity

Calvinist View: One of the elect could not be an enemy of the cross, as their desires are for the Cross.

Arminian Response: Those considered enemies of the cross may have once experienced God's grace, and have turned away to darkness.

Comment: It brings tears to the eyes of the Christian to see people live as enemies of the Cross. Since election is a category one shares by abiding in Christ, it is something that one may also depart from and become an enemy of it. This is hard for the Calvinist to believe, who understands salvation as pre-planned and set, so one may not wander out of it. For those who continue to abide in Christ there is no danger of becoming an enemy of God and the Cross.

Quick Points:

1) Actions and fruits can align a person with being an enemy of the Cross.

2) Abiding with/ in Christ is the only guarantee of not becoming an enemy of the Cross.

From the Experts:

"The characteristic of those persons mentioned in the following verse is, rather, that they were living in a manner which showed that they were strangers to his pure gospel. An immoral life is enmity to the cross of Christ; for he died to make us holy. A life where there is no evidence that the heart is renewed, is enmity to the cross; for he died that we might be renewed."
–Albert Barnes, *Barnes Notes on the Whole Bible*

The Bottom line: Abiding in Christ keeps one from being an enemy of the Cross.

Notes:

Colossians 1:21-23 (NIV)
[21] Once you were alienated from God and were enemies in your minds because of your evil behavior.
[22] But now he has reconciled you by Christ's physical body through death to present you holy in his sight, without blemish and free from accusation-
[23] if you continue in your faith, established and firm, not moved from the hope held out in the gospel. This is the gospel that you heard and that has been proclaimed to every creature under heaven, and of which I, Paul, have become a servant.

Context: God's reconciliation and Truth

Calvinist View: "Paul's statement to the Colossians seems to cast a shadow on the assurance of our future glory (see <u>Col. 1:23</u>). Is it possible for a believer to lose his salvation? No, the *if* clause does not suggest doubt or lay down a condition by which we "keep up our salvation."

Paul used an architectural image in this verse—a house, firmly set on the foundation. The town of Colossae was located in a region known for earthquakes, and the word translated "moved away" can mean "earthquake stricken." Paul was saying, "If you are truly saved, and built on the solid foundation, Jesus Christ, then you will continue in the faith and nothing will move you. You have heard the Gospel and trusted Jesus Christ, and He has saved you."

In other words, we are not saved by continuing in the faith. But we continue in the faith and thus prove that we are saved. It behooves each professing Christian to test his own faith and examine his own heart to be sure he is a child of God (<u>2 Cor. 13:5</u>; <u>2 Peter 1:10ff</u>)." –Warren Wiersbe, *Bible Exposition Commentary (BE Series) – New Testament, Volume 2.*

Arminian Response: Faith is necessary to remain in Christ.

Comment: Continuing in the faith does prove our faith as genuine, and ensures our standing in Christ.

Quick Points:

1) Continual faith is a sign of spiritual maturity and true love for God.

2) Faith keeps one from being moved, as it centers you in Christ.

From the Experts:

If ye continue in the faith – Otherwise, ye will lose all the blessings which ye have already begun to enjoy.

And be not removed from the hope of the gospel – The glorious hope of perfect love. –John Wesley, *Explanatory Notes upon the New Testament.*

The Bottom line: Continued faith is necessary to continue with God.

Notes:

Colossians 2:13 (NIV)

[13] When you were dead in your sins and in the uncircumcision of your sinful nature, God made you alive with Christ. He forgave us all our sins,

Context: Believer's Completeness in Christ

Calvinist View: The believer is made alive so he can believe (saved before saved).

Arminian Response: The seeker is courted by grace and made alive through regeneration (to born again through Christ), as they believe.

Comment: This is a general picture of how grace works, from sinner to repentant sinner being made alive in Christ. It is the natural result of believing– being made alive in Christ. For God to make you alive, you must first believe.

Quick Points:

1) It is God that makes the Christian spiritually alive.

2) Faith is not only a sign of spiritual maturity, but obedience to Christ.

From the Experts:

"We were dead, but God made us alive together with Christ." –*The Wesley Bible*

The Bottom line: God makes the believer alive in Him and forgiven, when they respond to grace by faith.

> ### Notes:

1 Thessalonians 5:9 (NIV)
[9] For God did not appoint us to suffer wrath but to receive salvation through our Lord Jesus Christ.

Context: The Believer in Conjunction with the Day of the Lord

Calvinist View: The elect are not appointed to be judged, but saved.

"As he has spoken of the hope of salvation, he follows out that department, and says that God has appointed us to this– that we may obtain salvation through Christ." –John Calvin, *Calvin's Commentaries on the Bible*

Arminian Response: God has called humans to be saved by faith, and not suffer the wrath that befalls sinners. Christians believing by faith and obeying have this promise.

Comment: God did not call humans to wrath, but salvation. Everyone is allowed to go down this route, but not all make the salvation choice. For these wrath has been appointed for their disobedience.

Quick Points:

1) God does not subject active believers to "wrath." The "us" were faithful believers.

2) The believer's calling is to salvation. Departure from it leads back to wrath.

From the Experts:

"Paul does not say that the human response of faith takes place in some men as a result of a divine decree, but only that God calls men powerfully by the Gospel."

"While, therefore, Paul teaches that divine choice is the basis of salvation, he does not teach that this choice reaches its goal without the faith of those called by the Gospel and their steadfast perseverance." –I. Howard Marshall, *Kept by the Power of God*

The Bottom line: The believer has made good on what was planned for them by God in ages past.

Notes:

2 Thessalonians 2:13 (NIV)
[13] But we ought always to thank God for you, brothers loved by the Lord, because from the beginning God chose you to be saved through the sanctifying work of the Spirit and through belief in the truth.

Context: Correcting a Misunderstanding

Calvinist View: The elect are secure from the beginning as they were chosen for salvation.

"…faith itself is produced only by the Spirit." –John Calvin, *Institutes of the Christian Religion.*

"Paul swept through the features of salvation, noting that believers are "beloved by the Lord" chosen for salvation from eternity past, set apart from sin by the Spirit, and called to eternal glory…They were destined for glory, not judgment, and would not be included with those deceived and judged in that Day." –John MacArthur, *The MacArthur Study Bible*

Arminian Response: God chose salvation to be issued to humanity by faith.

Comment: When a person believes they take up their position among the called/ elect, but are not part of a pre-selected group that cannot stop believing. A Christian stands up in election or their calling, but does not bypass faith in being chosen by God. He chooses particular people for certain offices and duties, but chooses all people to receive salvation.

Quick Points:

1) From the beginning God chose humans to partake in His salvation that would be bought by the Son and indwelt by the Spirit.

2) The planning out of salvation and the belief or faith in the truth, go hand in hand.

3) From the beginning salvation was planned, not decreed.

From the Experts:

"Here we note that God's calling comes to men through the preaching of the Gospel and is not something which takes place in past eternity." –I. Howard Marshall, *Kept by the Power of God*

"The meaning of "from the beginning" is the question. Paul uses this expression three other times: "who knew me from the beginning" Acts 25:6, "from the beginning of the world" (Ephesians 3:9); and in the beginning of the Gospel" (Philippians 4:15). None of these expressions is related to predestination from eternity past." –Dave Hunt, *Debating Calvinism*

The Bottom line: From the beginning God chose salvation to be accessible to the human race.

Notes:

1 Timothy 1:15 (NIV)

[15] Here is a trustworthy saying that deserves full acceptance: Christ Jesus came into the world to save sinners- of whom I am the worst.

Context: Dealing with False Doctrine

Calvinist View: Paul was saved because he was called to be elect. Jesus came to only save the elect.

Arminian Response: Paul was saved because he was a sinner responding by faith to God's grace.

Comment: Paul (initially called Saul) was a sinner saved by grace. Jesus came to save sinners. Those who believe fill out the ranks of the elect.

Quick Points:

1) Jesus came for sinners.

2) Paul confirmed his salvation invitation by believing.

From the Experts:

"**Came into the world to save sinners** – All sinners, without exception. –John Wesley, *Explanatory Notes upon the New Testament.*

"If he had died for only a part of the race, and could save only a part, it could not be said, with any propriety, that the doctrine was worthy of the acceptance of "all"." –Albert Barnes, *Notes on the New Testament Explanatory and Practical.*

The Bottom line: Jesus came for all sinners.

> **Notes:**
>
>

2 Timothy 1:9 (NIV)

[9] who has saved us and called us to a holy life- not because of anything we have done but because of his own purpose and grace. This grace was given us in Christ Jesus before the beginning of time,

Context: Dealing with False Doctrine

Calvinist View: Salvation is an exercise in sovereignty in which the Christian has been saved (from eternity past) and lives this calling out in faith. "The destiny of God's chosen was determined and sealed from eternity past." –John MacArthur, *The John MacArthur Study Bible*

" Although Paul commonly employs the word "purpose" to denote the secret decree of God, the cause of which is in his own power, yet, for the sake of fuller explanation, he chose to add "grace," –John Calvin, *John Calvin's Commentary on the Bible*

Arminian Response: God's purpose is for grace to reach out to humans and for them to respond in faith, thus be saved. They are called before by grace, but saved when they respond to grace.

Comment: Salvation is never based on anything we do. Responding to Christ's grace by faith is an act of obedience. That doesn't help gain salvation or gain points with God. God enables us to respond and helps us with faith. Since God provides the grace to enable us to have faith, it is not a work, just obedience.

Quick Points:

1) Salvation is from God start to finish.

2) The order is: grace calling us, humans responding by faith, salvation

3) Faith is responding to something God has done. The ability to have faith and believe are orchestrations of grace, not human works.

From the Experts:

"Having called us with an holy calling – Which is all from God, and claims us all for God." –John Wesley, *Explanatory Notes upon the New Testament.*

"And called us with a holy calling—Invited us to holiness and comfort here; and to eternal glory hereafter. Before the Mosaic dispensation took place, God purposed the salvation of the Gentiles by Christ Jesus; and the Mosaic dispensation was intended only as the introducer of the Gospel. The law was our schoolmaster unto Christ, Galatians 3:24." –Adam Clarke, *A Commentary and Critical Notes.*

"That is, which he intended to give us, for it was not then actually given. The thing was so certain in the Divine purposes that it might be said to be already done. Comp. Romans 4:17. –Albert Barnes, *Notes on the New Testament Explanatory and Practical.*

The Bottom line: Faith is the way that God's grace leads us into His planned and structured salvation.

> **Notes:**

2 Timothy 2:12 (NIV)

[12] if we endure, we will also reign with him. If we disown him, he will also disown us;

Context: The Believer's Union with Christ and Future Glory

Calvinist View:

"Speaks of a final, permanent denial, such as that of an apostate, not the temporary failure of a true believer, like Peter." –John MacArthur, *The MacArthur Study Bible*

Arminian Response:

"**If we endure**: Believers may rest assured of their salvation if they are faithful to Christ (Matt, 10:22). But it is possible to lose our salvation **if we deny him** (Matt. 10:33). –*The Wesley Bible*

Comment: Disowning Christ is not based on a few instances; it is the end of a long road of denial. Every Christian falters and fails in faith, but some lose their First Love (Revelation 2:4) and if they do not find Him again will be lost eternally.

Quick Points:

1) Rejection of Christ is not based on a few instances, but a life pattern.

2) Such rejection will ultimately end in eternal separation from God, if not repented of.

From the Experts:

"If we are; if we deny him in these things before people; if we are unwilling to express our attachment to him in every way possible, then it is right that he should "disown all connection with us," or deny us before God, and he will do it." –Albert Barnes, *Barnes Notes on the Whole Bible*

The Bottom line: Denying Christ is the opposite of living for Him.

2 Timothy 2:25 (NIV)

[25] Those who oppose him he must gently instruct, in the hope that God will grant them repentance leading them to a knowledge of the truth,

Context: Church Instructions

Calvinist View:

"When God, by grace, grants saving faith it includes the granting of repentance from sin. Neither is a human work." –John MacArthur, *The MacArthur Study Bible*

Arminian Response:

"He was to use every means which he had reason to believe God might bless; and the apostle intimates that, bad as they were, they were not out of the reach of God's mercy. –Adam Clarke, *A Commentary and Critical Notes.*

Comment: Correction of those in error needs to be done with humility. Such a Christ-like may lead the offenders into a state of repentance as God's grace works on them.

Quick Points:

1) All believers are saved by grace.

2) Instead of pride the believer's attitude in correcting should be cautious humility.

3) This attitude best reflects Christ and allows Him to work on souls.

From the Experts:

"He was to use every means which he had reason to believe God might bless; and the apostle intimates that, bad as they were, they were not out of the reach of God's mercy." –Adam Clarke, *A Commentary and Critical Notes*.

The Bottom line: Gentle correcting can lead souls back to Christ.

Notes:

Titus 3:5-7 (NIV)

[5] he saved us, not because of righteous things we had done, but because of his mercy. He saved us through the washing of rebirth and renewal by the Holy Spirit,
[6] whom he poured out on us generously through Jesus Christ our Savior,
[7] so that, having been justified by his grace, we might become heirs having the hope of eternal life.

Context: Prescribed Conduct of Believer's

Calvinist View:

"As works can't save, neither can they prove we are saved." –James White, *Debating Calvinism*

Arminian Response:

"In this important passage the apostle presents us with a delightful view of our redemption. Herein we have, The cause of it; not our works or righteousness, but "the kindness and love of God our Saviour." –John Wesley, *Explanatory Notes on the New Testament*

Comment: The believer is not saved by good works, but faith in Christ. God by His grace saves believers, faith is not a work. If a believer could believe without any grace from God, it would be a work towards salvation. But since faith is governed by free grace, it is not a work, but obedient response.

Quick Points:

1) Good deeds do not save the believer.

2) Faith does not fit in here as a deed, as God enables this faith, through His grace.

3) Apart from prevenient grace there would be no faith towards Christ.

From the Experts:

"Justification, in the gospel sense, is the free forgiveness of a sinner; accepting him as righteous through the righteousness of Christ received by faith. God, in justifying a sinner in the way of the gospel, is gracious to him, yet just to himself and his law. As forgiveness is through a perfect righteousness, and satisfaction is made to justice by Christ, it cannot be merited by the sinner himself. Eternal life is set before us in the promise; the Spirit works faith in us, and hope of that life; faith and hope bring it near, and fill with joy in expectation of it." –Matthew Henry, *Matthew Henry Concise Bible Commentary*.

The Bottom line: Good works do not save the believer, and should not be confused with grace given faith.

Notes:

Hebrews 6:4-6 (NIV)

[4] It is impossible for those who have once been enlightened, who have tasted the heavenly gift, who have shared in the Holy Spirit,
[5] who have tasted the goodness of the word of God and the powers of the coming age,
[6] if they fall away, to be brought back to repentance, because to their loss they are crucifying the Son of God all over again and subjecting him to public disgrace.

Context: The Superiority of Christ's Priesthood

Calvinist View: These are the people who never commit their lives to God, associated with the Holy Spirit, but not believing (John MacArthur).

"Those who believe in eternal security teach that this is an exhortation to the Jews in Jerusalem to not return to the temple to sacrifice a lamb for the forgiveness of sins." –Elmer Towns, *Bible Answers for Almost All Your Questions*

Arminian Response: These people were enlightened and had tasted of the things of God. Either belief comes out of freedom of choice, or it is forced by God per eternal decree. This Scripture portrays the one who believed and stopped believing.

Comment: It is hard for some to accept these verses as pertaining to believers as their whole system of salvation would then fall apart. The wording is clear and concise– these are believers. They knew God. They also were in a state of rejecting God. As long as they stayed in this position, there was no Sacrifice for them.

Quick Points:

1) The warnings of Scripture are not hypothetical.

2) The wording is that of believers.

3) Since they were actively rejecting the Sacrifice of Christ, no other sacrifice existed.

From the Experts:

"The word "tasted" is the same word used of Jesus in Heb. 2:9 when it is said that He "tasted death for every man," and means "to have full experience of." –Purkiser, *Security– The False & The True*

"Christians can backslide, tear down the foundation of repentance that is already laid. Should they again be admitted into the church, they will have to build again the foundation of repentance and do their first works again." –*Dake Annotated Bible*

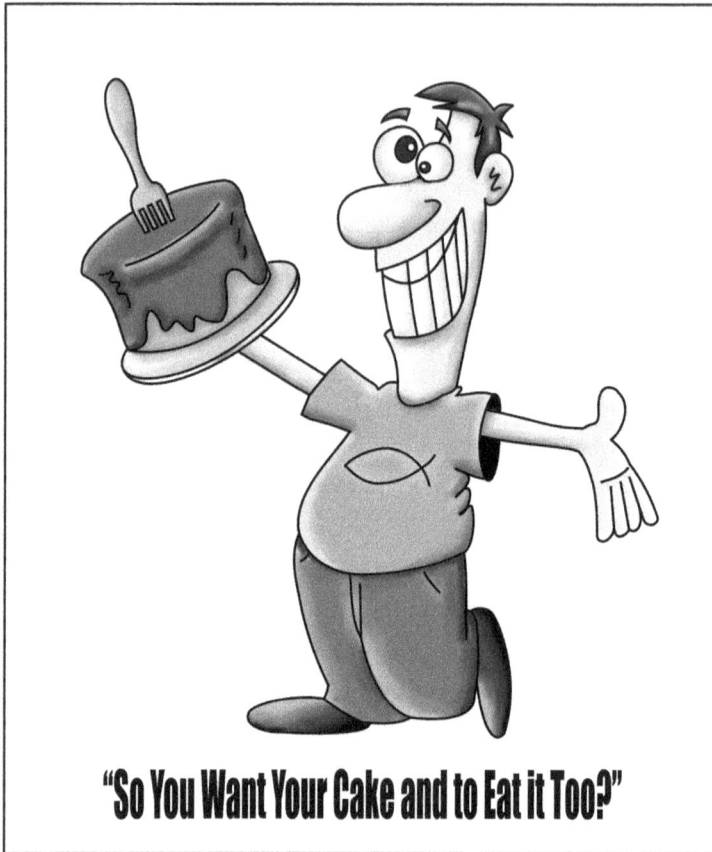

"So You Want Your Cake and to Eat it Too?"

"There is nothing here to exclude the possibility that Believers are being described…They had become sharers in the Holy Spirit. This is surely the mark of the Christian, and there is no place in the New Testament where an experience of the Spirit…is described here as attributed to people who were not Christians." –I. Howard Marshall, *Kept by the Power of God*

"There can be no doubt that these described are such as have been brought into living relationship with Christ. Of no unregenerate persons can it be said that they were "enlightened," "tasted of the heavenly gift," "tasted the good word of God, and the powers of the age to come." No person can be a partaker of the Holy Spirit save through faith in Jesus Christ, and all such are born again, and are members of Christ." –G. Campbell Morgan, *An Exposition of the Whole Bible*

The Bottom line: When people turn from the Cross, as long as they remain in their rebellion, there is no other sacrifice for them.

> **Notes:**

Hebrews 7:25 (NIV)
[25] Therefore he is able to save completely those who come to God through him, because he always lives to intercede for them.

Context: The Superior Priesthood of Christ

Calvinist View: Save completely means eternally called and secure. "When the writer asserted that **He is able to save completely,** he continued to have in mind the salvation–inheritance first referred to in 1:14. The readers were to hold fast to their professions of faith and to continue numbering themselves among **those who come to God through Him,** knowing that He can see them through every trial and difficulty right to the end of the road **because He always lives to intercede for them**" *—The Bible Knowledge Commentary: An Exposition of the Scriptures by Dallas Seminary Faculty.*

Arminian Response: No one gets to God but through Christ. He is certainly able to keep those who come and remain loyal to Him.

Comment: Salvation does not ever fail, as God is able through Christ to save us completely. Scripture says the He is "able to save completely" the believer. Security is indeed found in Christ, just not "out" of being in Christ.

Quick Points:

1) God's salvation is capable to save.

2) The fault falls on the follow through of the believer, who neglects the intercession and love of Christ.

From the Experts:

"Christ "is able to save them to the uttermost," but only those "come unto God by him" (Hebrews 7:25)." –Dave Hunt, *Debating Calvinism*

"*To the uttermost.* This does not mean simply *for ever*-but that he has power to save them so that their salvation shall be *complete*. He does not abandon the work midway; he does not begin a work which he is unable to finish. He can aid us *as long* as we need anything done for our salvation; he can save all who will entrust their salvation to his hands." –Albert Barnes, *Notes on the New Testament Explanatory and Practical.*

The Bottom line: Christ saves the believer thoroughly, any friction is not because of Him, but us.

Notes:

Hebrews 9:11-12 (NIV)

[11] When Christ came as high priest of the good things that are already here, he went through the greater and more perfect tabernacle that is not man-made, that is to say, not a part of this creation.
[12] He did not enter by means of the blood of goats and calves; but he entered the Most Holy Place once for all by his own blood, having obtained eternal redemption.

Context: The Superior Priesthood of Christ

Calvinist View: *Once for all* means your sins are forgiven and sin is stripped forever of power over you, thus you cannot lose salvation, just fellowship.

Arminian Response: Once for all is panoramic in scope, but conditional in application.

Comment: God had Jesus die for all sin, but leaves the application to sins once committed. You are not saved from the sin before, but after repentance. Salvation is conditional, based on the application of the Blood of Christ for unconfessed sin.

Quick Points:

1) Christ's sacrifice for sins on the Cross was done once to secure salvation past and present.

2) This victorious perfect sacrifice needs to be applied to sins as they are committed to bring the forgiveness from potential into action.

3) "Once for all" does not mean that sins do not need to be confessed and repented of, but the perfect sacrifice of the Savior we approach as we repent.

From the Experts:

"**For us** – All that believe."

–John Wesley, *Explanatory Notes upon the New Testament.*

"**Once**—Once for all, epsapadz εφαπαξ, in opposition to the annual entering of the high priest into the holiest, with the blood of the annual victim." –Adam Clarke, *A Commentary and Critical Notes.*

The Bottom line: Once for all is the qualitative nature of Christ's salvation.

Notes:

Hebrews 10:10, 14 (NIV)

[10] And by that will, we have been made holy through the sacrifice of the body of Jesus Christ once for all. [14] because by one sacrifice he has made perfect forever those who are being made holy.

Context: The Superior Priesthood of Christ

Calvinist View: Christ's sacrifice is complete (one for all) and is not contingent upon human faith. Sins are forgiven the first time one repents and further repentance is not necessary for salvation.

"We say Christ so died that he infallibly secured the salvation of a multitude that no man can number, who through Christ's death not only may be saved, but cannot by any possibility run the hazard of being anything but saved (Charles Spurgeon)." –James White, *Debating Calvinism*

Arminian Response: Christ died for our sins once (complete) instead of ongoing (incomplete). He died for all sins (in scope and activity), but this provision is conditional being based on repentance when sins are committed. Forgiveness is enacted when the believer repents.

Comment: Christ died once to perfectly bring us salvation, and end the endless cycle of Old Testament sacrifices for forgiveness of sins. This perfectly capable provision is waiting to be applied to our sins. Each sin is to be repented of as it is known to be forgiven.

Quick Points:

1) *Once for all* speaks to the finality of Christ's work on the Cross.

2) God's plan is for us to find an Advocate in Christ, as we sin and need forgiveness (1 John 2:1).

3) The salvation of a believer is perfect (once for all sacrifice) and being perfected (spiritual formation and application) as it is lives out and applied.

From the Experts:

"…it perfects those who are being sanctified." –Dave Hunt, *Debating Calvinism*

"What then remains, but that we seek an interest in this Sacrifice by faith; and the seal of it to our souls, by the sanctification of the Spirit unto obedience? So that by the law being written in our hearts, we may know that we are justified, and that God will no more remember our sins." –Matthew Henry, *Matthew Henry Concise Bible Commentary*.

The Bottom line: Christ's sacrifice for sin is complete and is to be applied to each instance of sin.

> **Notes:**

Hebrews 10:26-29 (NIV)

[26] If we deliberately keep on sinning after we have received the knowledge of the truth, no sacrifice for sins is left,
[27] but only a fearful expectation of judgment and of raging fire that will consume the enemies of God.
[28] Anyone who rejected the law of Moses died without mercy on the testimony of two or three witnesses.
[29] How much more severely do you think a man deserves to be punished who has trampled the Son of God under foot, who has treated as an unholy thing the blood of the covenant that sanctified him, and who has insulted the Spirit of grace?

Context: The Superiority of Christ's Faith

Calvinist View: They received the knowledge of the truth but were not true believers. "He shows how severe a vengeance of God awaits all those who fall away from the grace of Christ; for being without that one true salvation, they are now as it were given up to an inevitable destruction." –John Calvin, *Calvin's Commentary on the Bible*

"The apostate is beyond salvation because he has rejected the only sacrifice that can cleanse him from sin and bring him into God's presence." –John MacArthur, *The MacArthur Study Bible*

"...this verse is a reference to Jews in the first century who attempted to go back to the Old Testament temple in Jerusalem to sacrifice a lamb to get forgiveness of sins." –Elmer Towns, *Bible Answers for Almost All Your Questions*

Arminian Response: They had knowledge of the truth and desired to keep on sinning. There is no sacrifice for those who want to sin instead of receive forgiveness of sins.

Comment: A human may taste of the things of God and knowledge of the truth and yet walk away from him. The danger for the Jewish believers was to return to the Law, and either mix Christ and the Law, or just plain return to the Law. Such actions would be trampling Christ's sacrifice, and leaving no hope while remaining in this mode.

Quick Points:

1) It is possible to taste of God and yet leave.

2) Either God makes salvation gracious enough to take or leave, or He imputes it and there is no choice only mechanical implementation. Scripture speaks of grace.

3) Rejection of the Sacrifice of Christ leaves no other hope for the individual.

From the Experts:

"The verb tense is present. While we are sinning willfully there after having received the knowledge of the truth, there is no sacrifice for sins." –Purkiser, *Security– The False & The True*

"Those who are in danger have received the knowledge of the truth (Hebrews 10:26), a phrase which refers to acceptance of the truth at conversion or to renewal of Christian experience after conversion. They are also described as having been enlightened (Hebrews 10:32)." –I. Howard Marshall, *Kept By the Power of God*

"...strongly forbids any assumption of the irresistibility of grace." –Robert Shank, *Elect in the Son*

The Bottom line: Just as there is no other name to be saved under (Acts 4:12), so also there is no other sacrifice, but Christ's to respond to. Failure to do so is spiritually fatal.

> **Notes:**

Hebrews 10:38 (NIV)

[38] But my righteous one will live by faith. And if he shrinks back, I will not be pleased with him."

Context: Warnings against abandoning Jesus, the Son of God

Calvinist View:

"From self-security, insolence, and contempt, it comes that as long as it is well with the wicked, they dare, as one has said, to insult the clouds. But since nothing is more contrary to faith than this drawing back, for the true character of faith is, that it draws a man unto submission to God when drawn back by his own sinful nature." –John Calvin, *Commentary on the Bible*

Arminian Response:

"**By faith** – As long as he retains that gift of God.

But if he draw back – If he make shipwreck of his faith

My soul hath no pleasure in him – That is, I abhor him; I cast him off. Habakkuk 2:3, etc." –John Wesley, *Explanatory Notes upon the New Testament.*

Comment: The righteous in the Bible always lived by faith. This did not mean that they did not fail or make mistakes or sin. They did remain heading in the right direction– God's direction. Those who stopped follow and started off on their own leave this faithful journey. Of such, God is not pleased.

Quick Points:

1) The believer is intended to live by faith.

2) Unbelief is not an option.

3) Shrinking back brings displeasure with God, and is to be avoided.

From the Experts:

"**the just:** Those in right relationship to God. Their way of life is determined by their faith." –*The Wesley Bible*

The Bottom line: Faith is not insignificant or a byproduct of salvation, but glued into the mix by God.

Notes:

Hebrews 12:1, 2 (NIV)
[1] Therefore, since we are surrounded by such a great cloud of witnesses, let us throw off everything that hinders and the sin that so easily entangles, and let us run with perseverance the race marked out for us. [2] Let us fix our eyes on Jesus, the author and perfecter of our faith, who for the joy set before him endured the cross, scorning its shame, and sat down at the right hand of the throne of God.

Context: The Superior Faith of Christ

Calvinist View:

"The reference is to those Hebrews who had made a profession of Christ, but had not gone all the way to full faith. They had not yet the race which starts with salvation." –John MacArthur, *The John MacArthur Study Bible*

Arminian Response: This passage shows the perfect salvation that was purchased on the Cross. It is accessed by faith of the individual in Christ. It addresses believers– "Let us."

Comment: The believers that have gone ahead and paved the way stand as a great cloud of witnesses, encouraging all who come behind. Anything that hinders or sin that entangles is to be avoided. Sin can still be powerfully detrimental to the believer and though forgiveness has been provided, unconfessed sin can still lead to falling away.

Quick Points:

1) Believers in the past encourage us with their godly example.

2) There are things that can make the believer lose out: snares that lead to sin.

From the Experts:

"He is at the head of all those who have furnished an example of confidence in God, for he was himself the most illustrious instance of it. The expression, then, does not mean properly that he produces faith in us, or that we believe because he causes us to believe—whatever may be the truth about that–but that he stands at the head as the most eminent example that can be referred to on the subject of faith." –Albert Barnes, *Notes on the New Testament Explanatory and Practical.*

The Bottom line: Jesus completed what God started

Notes:

James 5:19-20 (NIV)

[19] My brothers, if one of you should wander from the truth and someone should bring him back,

[20] remember this: Whoever turns a sinner from the error of his way will save him from death and cover over a multitude of sins.

Context: Living Faith seen in an Active Witness

Calvinist View:

"…those professing believers who have strayed from the truth." –John MacArthur, *The MacArthur Study Bible*

Arminian Response: James was writing to Christians (My brothers, "one of you"), and Christians leading Christians back to life everlasting.

Comment: It is obvious from the text that the believer in the formula was considered to have "wandered" from the truth to the point of this being a critical issue. It could lead to not just temporal losses, but eternal. Since all sinners are grace-saved, restoring another believer needs to be done with a humble, cautious attitude.

Quick Points:

1) Believers wander from the faith.

2) Other believers need to guard themselves, as they humbly restore another.

From the Experts:

"It is a brother who has erred. Not a false professor, but a real Christian. He is to be converted like any other sinner. If not converted, his soul is in danger of death." –Bishop B.T. Roberts, *Holiness Teachings*

"A brother may wander from the truth into sin and error. In this case it is the duty of his Christian brothers to bring him back. Such an act, if successful, is regarded as "saving his soul from death and covering a multitude of sins." The former of these results shows that the backslider was in danger of eternal condemnation at God's judgment; for something more than a physical penalty is surely meant. If a backslider does not confess his sin and repent, he becomes a witting sinner and is in danger of loss of salvation." –I. Howard Marshall, *Kept By the Power of God*

The Bottom line: If a believer wanders other Christians need to tenderly, gracefully restore them.

Notes:

1 Peter 1:1 (NIV)

[1] Peter, an apostle of Jesus Christ, To God's elect, strangers in the world, scattered throughout Pontus, Galatia, Cappadocia, Asia and Bithynia,

Context: Encouragement in Suffering

Calvinist View: God's elect– those picked for eternal salvation.

"…those chosen by God for salvation." – John MacArthur, *The MacArthur Study Bible*

Arminian Response: God's elect– those who are believers and have stepped into that category by faith.

Comment: "God the Father has chosen those who believe to be His own special possession." –*The Wesley Bible*

Quick Points:

1) The elect are those who faithfully believe on Jesus for salvation.

2) To be elect is to be an active believer.

3) Election is not like a necklace that can be worn without, having recognizable and like qualities of the elect in Scripture.

"Arrr...what do ya mean, Swabbie,
that I'm not acting elect? Why I'll..."

From the Experts:

"The elect are objects of the action of God and members of the resultant state or status. The elect are those whom God has "elected," and the basis for this divine choice is in the moral character which they have been enabled, through God's transforming grace, to embody, and experience." –*Beacon Dictionary of Theology*

"By the free love and almighty power of God taken out of, separated from, the world. Election, in the scripture sense, is God's doing anything that our merit or power have no part in. The true predestination, or foreappointment of God is,

1. He that believeth shall be saved from the guilt and power of sin.

2. He that endureth to the end shall be saved eternally.

3. They who receive the precious gift of faith, thereby become the sons of God; and, being sons, they shall receive the Spirit of holiness to walk as Christ also walked.

Throughout every part of this appointment of God, promise and duty go hand in hand. All is free gift; and yet such is the gift, that the final issue depends on our future obedience to the heavenly call. But other predestination than this, either to life or death eternal, the scripture knows not of." –John Wesley, *Explanatory Notes upon the NT*

The Bottom line: The elect are believers who hold an active licensed by God election.

> **Notes:**

1 Peter 1:3-5 (NIV)

[3] Praise be to the God and Father of our Lord Jesus Christ! In his great mercy he has given us new birth into a living hope through the resurrection of Jesus Christ from the dead, [4] and into an inheritance that can never perish, spoil or fade- kept in heaven for you, [5] who through faith are shielded by God's power until the coming of the salvation that is ready to be revealed in the last time.

Context: Looking Back on God's Great Salvation

Calvinist View: The inheritance does not spoil or fade, and they are shielded because they are inseparable from Christ due to election and predestination.

"Supreme power, omniscience, omnipotence, and sovereignty, not only keep the inheritance (v.4), but also keep the believer secure. No one can steal the Christian's treasure, and no one can disqualify him from receiving it. The Christian's response to God's election and the Spirit's conviction is faith, but even faith is empowered by God." – John MacArthur, *The MacArthur Study Bible*

Arminian Response: The quality and duration of salvation is in focus here. This is what the believer receives, who is "in Christ." The believer is kept by the power of God, through faith and is then saved. Without faith the equation falls apart. God does not make one believe to His end, but uses people who believe.

Comment: Salvation does not spoil or perish. It is kept by God. The key word here, by "faith," is shielded by God's power.

Quick Points:

1) God keeps salvation safe as well as believers (believing).

2) They are shielded "through faith."

3) Such a state brings true security.

From the Experts:

"The true disciples of Christ are under the continual watchful care of God, and the inheritance is guarded for them." –Adam Clarke, *A Commentary and Critical Notes*.

"If we continue to trust in Christ, God's power will enable us to receive this salvation when it is revealed in its fullness ay Christ's return." –*The Wesley Bible*

The Bottom line: Faithful believers are kept safe and secure.

Notes:

1 Peter 1:22-25 (NIV)

[22] Now that you have purified yourselves by obeying the truth so that you have sincere love for your brothers, love one another deeply, from the heart.
[23] For you have been born again, not of perishable seed, but of imperishable, through the living and enduring word of God.
[24] For, "All men are like grass, and all their glory is like the flowers of the field; the grass withers and the flowers fall,
[25] but the word of the Lord stands forever." And this is the word that was preached to you.

Context: Looking Back on God's Great Salvation

Calvinist View: Being born again is imperishable, meaning it cannot go away ever.

"The spiritual life implanted by the Holy Spirit to produce the new birth is unfailing and permanent." –John MacArthur, *The MacArthur Study Bible*

Arminian Response: Imperishable means that God has crafted it to last. The focus is on the quality of the product, not the holder of it.

Comment: Born again is imperishable and the Word is forever established. Can the Believer walk into an irreversible position by being born again? God's grace, love, and justice would say no.

Quick Points:

1) Being born again is by imperishable means.

2) Faith leads the believer into a conditional salvation forged imperishable in quality and capability.

3) It works just fine, it is the believer that loses faith and way.

From the Experts:

The soul must be purified, before it can give up its own desires and indulgences. And the word of God planted in the heart by the Holy Ghost, is a means of spiritual life, stirring up to our duty, working a total change in the dispositions and affections of the soul, till it brings to eternal life. –Matthew Henry, *Matthew Henry Concise Bible Commentary*.

The Bottom line: The new born again life is incorruptable, but the Christians relation to that life is conditioned in Christ.

> **Notes:**

2 Peter 2:1 (NIV)

[1] But there were also false prophets among the people, just as there will be false teachers among you. They will secretly introduce destructive heresies, even denying the sovereign Lord who bought them- bringing swift destruction on themselves.

Context: Reflecting on Christ's Example

Calvinist View: The sovereign Lord refers to the decree for Christ to die for the elect. The false prophets would prove they were not true believers.

"They are probably claiming that they were Christians, so that the Lord had bought them actually and personally." –John MacArthur, *The MacArthur Study Bible*

Arminian Response: God solely put our salvation package together, and it is God who offers and enable faith in Him. The false prophets were offered grace but refused to submit.

Comment: God sovereignly planned and brought salvation through Christ. The false teachers diluted the truth mixing it with error. This did not mean they were called to be reprobate, but that they chose to avoid the Truth by God given freewill.

Quick Points:

1) God perfectly offers salvation to all.

2) Evil desires draw people away, not God.

From the Experts:

"They first, by denying the Lord, introduced destructive heresies, that is, divisions; or they occasioned first these divisions, and then were given up to a reprobate mind, even to deny the Lord that bought them. Either the heresies are the effect of denying the Lord, or the denying the Lord was the consequence of the heresies," –John Wesley, *Explanatory Notes upon the New Testament.*

The Bottom line: All are given an opportunity to share grace evenly (evem false prophets).

Notes:

2 Peter 2:14, 18-22 (NIV)

[14] With eyes full of adultery, they never stop sinning; they seduce the unstable; they are experts in greed- an accursed brood! [18] For they mouth empty, boastful words and, by appealing to the lustful desires of sinful human nature, they entice people who are just escaping from those who live in error. [19] They promise them freedom, while they themselves are slaves of depravity- for a man is a slave to whatever has mastered him.
[20] If they have escaped the corruption of the world by knowing our Lord and Savior Jesus Christ and are again entangled in it and overcome, they are worse off at the end than they were at the beginning.
[21] It would have been better for them not to have known the way of righteousness, than to have known it and then to turn their backs on the sacred command that was passed on to them.
[22] Of them the proverbs are true: "A dog returns to its vomit," and, "A sow that is washed goes back to her wallowing in the mud."

Context: Knowing Who the Enemy is

Calvinist View: This refers to a person who knew of God, but proved they were not elect by not staying.

"They [false teachers– emphasis added] professed the Christian experience (the way of righteousness), and even had access to the true teachings of Scripture." –John MacArthur, *The MacArthur Study Bible*

Arminian Response: Such a person knew the way of righteousness (at a heart level), and turned their back on it. They did not remain in it, but they tasted the things of God.

Comment: Peter poses a hypothetical situation of sinful persons having escaped sin for a time, finding shelter in Jesus, and then being entangled again. If they were entangled "again" then there was a period of un-entanglement in Christ. They are now worse off, because they had known and experienced the truth, but chose to live in error. The soul that departs from Christ will forever be haunted by "the way of righteousness." The hound of heaven will relentlessly pursue the prodigal on the run.

Quick Points:

1) The persons in the text had known the way of righteousness, having had a lapse from sinning.

2) This was not their current state.

3) They had to live with this reality.

From the Experts:

"**Through the knowledge of Christ** – That is, through faith in him, 2 Peter 1:3. They are again entangled therein, and overcome, **their last state is worse than the first** – More inexcusable, and causing a greater damnation." –John Wesley, *Explanatory Notes upon the New Testament.*

"But if, after having been healed, and escaped the death to which we were exposed, we get again entangled, εμπλακεντες emplakentedz, enfolded, enveloped with them; then the latter end will be worse than the beginning: forasmuch as we shall have sinned against more light, and the soul, by its conversion to God, having had all its powers and faculties greatly improved, is now, being repolluted, more capable of iniquity than before, and can bear more expressively the image of the earthly. –Adam Clarke, *A Commentary and Critical Notes.*

The Bottom line: The sinner who experiences grace, but walks away is worse than never having known it.

> **Notes:**

1 John 1:5-6 (NIV)

[5] This is the message we have heard from him and declare to you: God is light; in him there is no darkness at all.

[6] If we claim to have fellowship with him yet walk in the darkness, we lie and do not live by the truth.

Context: The Conditions Linked to Fellowship

Calvinist View: God decreed for the non-elect to go to Hell, and this pleased His holy nature. "All are not created on equal terms, but some are preordained to eternal life, others to eternal damnation; and, accordingly, as each has been created for one or other of these ends, we say that he has been predestinated to life or to death." (Book Three, Chapter 21) "...that whenever God is pleased to make way for his providence, he even in external matters so turns and bends the wills of men, that whatever the freedom of their choice may be, it is still subject to the disposal of God." (Book Two, Chapter 4) "He teaches that salvation is prepared for those only on whom the Lord is pleased to bestow his mercy—that ruin and death await all whom he has not chosen." (Book Two, Chapter 5) "If this is the nature of the promises, let us now see whether there be any inconsistency between the two things—viz. that God, by an eternal decree, fixed the number of those whom he is pleased to embrace in love, and on whom he is pleased to display his wrath, and that he offers salvation indiscriminately to all. I hold that they are perfectly consistent, for all that is meant by the promise is, just that his mercy is offered to all who desire and implore it, and this none do, save those whom he has enlightened. Moreover, he enlightens those whom he has predestinated to salvation." (Book Three, Chapter 24) –John Calvin, *Institutes of the Christian Religion*.

Arminian Response: There is no darkness in God. For God to make humans do evil would make Him a dark being, or be set under damnation before even sinning would be evil. "The source of wisdom, knowledge, holiness, and happiness; and in him is no darkness at all—no ignorance, no imperfection, no sinfulness, no misery. –Adam Clarke, *A Commentary and Critical Notes*.

Comment: If a Believer does not match their talk to their walk consistently–something is wrong. It may be they are not yet saved. It may be that they are struggling with sin. It may be that their heart has departed from God. The term "Christian" defines a life following and seeking to reflect God. Walking in darkness is not doing this. This verse reminds us that God is not the author or administrator of evil in any way, shape, or form. God has not planned to save some and damn others to Hell to please Him.

Quick Points:

1) God can do no evil (i.e. plan to damn souls who will never have a chance to choose Him non-elect).

2) God as light wants to shine His light in a warm beckoning manner, not to blind those He never intended to save.

3) Jesus is the Light of the world (the whole world).

From the Experts:

"Our actions prove, that the truth is not in us." –John Wesley, *Explanatory Notes on the NT*

"Now if a man profess to have such communion, and walk in darkness—live an irreligious and sinful life, he lies, in the profession which he makes, and does not the truth—does not walk according to the directions of the Gospel, on the grace of which he holds his relation to God, and his communion with him." –Adam Clarke, *A Commentary and Critical Notes*.

The language is probably designed to guard the mind from an error to which it is prone, that of charging God with being the Author of the sin and misery which exist on the earth; and the apostle seems to design to teach that whatever was the source of sin and misery, it was not in any sense to be charged on God. –Albert Barnes, *Notes on the New Testament Explanatory and Practical.*

"Light and darkness are to be understood ethically rather than metaphysically: "light" is a synonym of goodness and truth, while "darkness" is a synonym of evil and falsehood." –F. F. Bruce, *The Gospel & Epistles of John.*

The Bottom line: If we lie and do not live by the truth, we do not live with God.

> **Notes:**

1 John 2:19 (NIV)

[19] They went out from us, but they did not really belong to us. For if they had belonged to us, they would have remained with us; but their going showed that none of them belonged to us.

Context: Knowing Who the Enemy is

Calvinist View:

"It is not strange that God should be implacable to those whom John, in his Epistle, declares not to have been of the elect, from whom they went out (1 John 2:19)." John Calvin, *Institutes of the Christian Religion.*

"The verse also places emphasis on the doctrine of the perseverance of the saints. Those genuinely born again endure in faith and fellowship and the truth." –John MacArthur, *The MacArthur Study Bible*

Arminian Response:

"**They were not of us** – When they went; their hearts were before departed from God, otherwise, they would have continued with us: but they went out,

that they might be made manifest – That is, this was made manifest by their going out. –John Wesley, *Explanatory Notes upon the New Testament.*

Comment: It seems pretty much unanimous that those in question were heretics. Paths part over if they ever believed and were they set under judgment before the fact. Calvinists would say they did not really believe, and never had a chance. Arminians would say they believed to a point, and by their works proved their faith had died. Such do not belong to the church in their current state.

Quick Points:

1) Even heretics may have believed at some point in Christ by faith.

2) Their lack of faith and obedience proves they are not following the narrow path (Matthew 7:14) of Christ.

From the Experts:

"These heretics had belonged to our Christian assemblies, they professed Christianity, and do so still; but we apostles did not commission them to preach to you, for they have disgraced the Divine doctrine with the most pernicious opinions; they have given up or explained away its most essential principles; they have mingled the rest with heathenish rites and Jewish glosses." –Adam Clarke, *A Commentary and Critical Notes.*

"*They went out from us.* From the church. That is, they had once been professors of the religion of the Saviour, though their apostasy showed that they never had any true piety." –Albert Barnes, *Notes on the New Testament Explanatory and Practical.*

The Bottom line: Heretics diprove themselves by the absence of faith and proper works.

> Notes:

1 John 2:25 (NIV)

[25] And this is what he promised us- even eternal life.

Context: Fellowship Companions

Calvinist View: God does not promise eternal life if it will not indeed be eternal for its recipients. "The sum of what is said is, that we cannot live otherwise than by nourishing to the end the seed of life sown in our hearts. John insists much on this point, that not only the beginning of a blessed life is to be found in the knowledge of Christ, but also its perfection." –John Calvin, *Commentary on the Bible*

Arminian Response: Eternal life is eternal for those who remain in Christ. It's substance and duration is not affected by humans.

Comment: Salvation has been promise and planned for humans from before time. God is capable of seeing things through, it just comes down to the human. God uses freewill as a stage to let salvation play out or stop dead in its tracks.

Quick Points:

1) Salvation has been promised to humans.

2) Those who take hold of it become Christians.

3) They begin eternal life on earth conditionally, that can continue into eternity if their faith persists on Earth.

From the Experts:

"Hath promised us – If we abide in him." –John Wesley, *Explanatory Notes upon the New Testament.*

"John's readers will do well if they hold fast to the message and remain in the fellowship, without which eternal life is unattainable." –F.F. Bruce, *The Gospel & Epistles of John*

The Bottom line: Eternal life is promised to those who will receive Jesus Christ as Lord.

Notes:

1 John 2:29 (NIV)
[29] If you know that he is righteous, you know that everyone who does what is right has been born of him.

Context: Fellowship Companions

Calvinist View: The elect are righteous , and they will do what is right. "In effect John is saying that God's children look like the Father - they take after their Father. If they don't take after the Father, they must not be the Father's children." –J. Vernon McGee, *Thru The Bible with J. Vernon McGee.*

Arminian Response: The righteous do what is right, which proves they are born again.

Comment: Who does right? Only those who have been lifted by grace from "doing no right," to being made right. Everyone who is born of him does right. Being born again is the key that places one in the "elect" category, fulfilling what has been set in ages past.

Quick Points:

1) The righteous are born into position.

2) They do what is right because they are set right.

From the Experts:

"Is born of him – For all his children are like himself." –John Wesley, *Explanatory Notes upon the New Testament.*

"Then, let us beware of holding the truth in unrighteousness, remembering that those only are born of God, who bear his holy image, and walk in his most righteous ways." –Matthew Henry, *Matthew Henry Concise Bible Commentary.*

The Bottom line: To be born of Jesus is to be able to do what is right, and please God.

> **Notes:**

1 John 3:9 (NIV)
[9] No one who is born of God will continue to sin, because God's seed remains in him; he cannot go on sinning, because he has been born of God.

Context: What Fellowship is Marked with

Calvinist View: This is the elect person, born of God, who struggles with the war between the flesh and spirit.

"remains" The word conveys the idea of the permanence of the new birth which cannot be reversed" –John MacArthur, *The MacArthur Study Bible*

Arminian Response: The Christian, born of God, exhibits fruit of yielding to God and avoiding patterns of sin. The process is made easier when Entire Sanctification cleanses the sin nature.

Comment: Everyone makes a mistake or bad choice leading into sin, but only the soul that is toying with sin lives in cycles of sin. The soul that loves God does not toy with sin like this.

Quick Points:

1) Cycles of sin is what John is looking at here.

2) The Christ born son of God does not NEED to sin in thought, word, and deed.

From the Experts:

"This does not say that the child of God is not able to sin. What it says is that he is able not to sin. The seed of God and the principle of sin are logically contradictory moral qualities, just as truthfulness and lying, patriotism and treason– and cannot exist together." –Purkiser, *Freedom– The False & The True*

"Once again, John emphasizes that the practice of sin is something that characterizes the children of him who "has been sinning from the beginning" (v.8), not the children of God." –F.F. Bruce, *The Gospel & Epistles of John*

The Bottom line: Sinning as a routine and loving God are heading in two different directions.

Notes:

1 John 3:10 (NIV)

[10] This is how we know who the children of God are and who the children of the devil are: Anyone who does not do what is right is not a child of God; nor is anyone who does not love his brother.

Context: Fellowship's Markings

Calvinist View: The child of the devil is the person who has never been saved.

"But he does not mean that they are thus manifested, so as to be openly recognized by the whole world; but his meaning is only this, that the fruit and adoption always appear in the life." –John Calvin, *Calvin's Commentary on the Bible*

Arminian Response: The "child of the devil" is a title earned by ongoing behavior and state of heart, and can refer to a "once" believer that has vacated their residence of faith.

Comment: Sometimes people say works are not important, or they say that believers just naturally do the right works because they have to by decree of God. The truth is that believers reflect God because they choose to per freewill. Those who do not do right also choose per freewill to do such works.

Quick Points:

1) Works prove or disprove humans as believers.

2) Sinful works prove one is not being obedient to God.

3) Though some may argue about the status of one's salvation, they would not disagree that negative works disintegrate fellowship with God.

From the Experts:

"Once a son, always a son," it is argued. But this metaphor proves too much. It proves that we can never be saved in the first place, for we were all born "children of wrath" (Eph. 2:3), and "children of the devil" (1 John 3:10). If once born into a family we could never cease to be children of that family, then we must always be children of disobedience." –Purkiser, *Security– The False & The True*

"For him, righteousness and love are inseparable; since they are inseparable in the character of God and in His revelation in Christ, so they must be inseparable in the lives of His people." –F.F. Bruce, *The Gospel & Epistles of John*

The Bottom line: Wicked works show the true condition of the heart.

> **Notes:**

1 John 4:7 (NIV)

[7] Dear friends, let us love one another, for love comes from God. Everyone who loves has been born of God and knows God.

Context: Marks of Fellowship

Calvinist View: The elect child of God is naturally full of God's love. "When he commands *mutual* love, he does not mean that we discharge this duty when we love our friends, because they love us; but as he addresses in common the faithful, he could not have spoken otherwise than that they were to exercise mutual love." –John Calvin, *Calvin's Commentary on the Bible*

Arminian Response: God's love in one's heart is evidence of being born again and being elect by faith.

Comment: Love is a fruit that cannot be faked for long. Agape, selfless love, comes from the Holy Spirit in the heart of a believer and proves genuine experience. This is why love is so important to God (1 John 4).

Quick Points:

1) God's love in humans is a good indicator they know Him.

2) This love is to be selfless, God-seeking love, not "eros" self-seeking love.

From the Experts:

"Those who show such love to one another give proof in doing so that they are God's children and that it is they who really know him. Those, on the other hand, from whose lives such love is absent give proof by that fact that they have never begun to know God, however confident their claims may be." –F.F. Bruce, *The Gospel & Epistles of John*

The Bottom line: Selfless love reflects God in humans.

> **Notes:**
>
>
>
>
>

1 John 4:19 (NIV)
[19] We love because he first loved us.

Context: Proving Fellowship

Calvinist View:

"…the Apostle, as I think, repeats the preceding sentence, that as God has anticipated us by his free love, we ought to return to render love to him, for he immediately infers that he ought to be loved in men, or that the love we have for him ought to be manifested towards men." –John Calvin, *Calvin's Commentary on the Bible*

Arminian Response: God's love always goes before ours, and this same love can graciously become ours.

Comment: Reflecting God includes reflecting His love. The believer is able to do this, because God first did this to them.

Quick Points:

1) Love traces back to God.

2) The believer who loves has been influenced and changed by God, to take on His image.

From the Experts:

"In taking the initiative in loving us, He not only showed us how to love one another but He imparted the desire and the power to follow this example of His." –F.F. Bruce, *The Gospel & Epistles of John*

The Bottom line: Love in the life of the believer comes from God.

Notes:

1 John 5:1 (NIV)

[1] Everyone who believes that Jesus is the Christ is born of God, and everyone who loves the father loves his child as well.

Context: Assurance of Fellowship with God

Calvinist View:

"The new birth brings us into a permanent faith relationship with God and Christ." –John MacArthur, *The MacArthur Study Bible*

"Hence the Apostle declares that all they who really believe have been born of God; for faith is far above the reach of the human mind, so that we must be drawn to Christ by our heavenly Father; for not any of us can ascend to him by his own strength." –John Calvin, *Calvin's Commentary on the Bible*

Regeneration precedes faith in Christ unto salvation.

"…the tense of born points us to a preceding, determining, divine action that then results in the ongoing actions noted." –James White, *Debating Calvinism*

Arminian Response:

"Every one who loveth God that begat loveth him also that is begotten of him – Hath a natural affection to all his brethren." –John Wesley, *Explanatory Notes upon the New Testament.*

Comment: "Everyone" who believes. Salvation is open ended, and yet God knows who will endure and remain. All will not be saved, and yet all are given the same invitation (Rec. 3:20) and mercies.

Quick Points:

1) Notice the Biblical flow– belief, then born of God, and love for God and then others.

2) Believers are not born of God before believing.

From the Experts:

"If, in the proper sense of the phrase, a man does believe that Jesus *is the Christ*, receiving him as he is revealed as the Anointed of God, and a Saviour, it is undoubtedly true that that constitutes him a Christian, for that is what is required of a man in order that he may be saved. –Albert Barnes, *Notes on the New Testament Explanatory and Practical.*

"Faith is the cause of victory, the means, the instrument, the spiritual armour by which we overcome. In and by faith we cleave to Christ, in contempt of, and in opposition to the world." –Matthew Henry, *Matthew Henry Concise Bible Commentary.*

The Bottom line: Belief on Jesus as Lord leads to salvation,

Notes:

1 John 5:12-13 (NIV)

[12] He who has the Son has life; he who does not have the Son of God does not have life.

[13] I write these things to you who believe in the name of the Son of God so that you may know that you have eternal life.

Context: Assurance of Fellowship with God

Calvinist View: The elect have life and are in Christ, a position they will not depart from.

"Life is only in Him, so it is impossible to have it without Him." –John MacArthur, *The MacArthur Study Bible*

"those who have no part in Christ, whoever they be, whatever they do or devise, are hastening on, during their whole career, to destruction and the judgment of eternal death. For this reason, Augustine says, "Our religion distinguishes the righteous from the wicked, by the law, not of works but of faith, without which works which seem good are converted into sins," –John Calvin, *Institutes of the Christian Religion.*

Arminian Response:

"**he that hath not the Son of God hath not this life** – Hath no part or lot therein. In the former clause, the apostle says simply, the Son; because believers know him: in the latter, the Son of God; that unbelievers may know how great a blessing they fall short of. –John Wesley, *Explanatory Notes upon the New Testament.*

Comment: Pretty simple. If you have Jesus you have life. If you don't– you don't. But it goes deeper. Not having the Son implies– not obeying, not seeking, and not selflessly abiding in Him. There comes a point in the life of a Believer if you do not "have" the Son in these points, then you are deluded and believing in a cruel fairy tale. Seeking to bear the Son's name only for security and not fellowship, is not really having the Son.

Quick Points:

1) Life in the Son comes by faith.

2) No life, no Son.

3) This applies to believer believing, not believing.

From the Experts:

"It plainly follows, **he that hath the Son** – Living and reigning in him by faith." –John Wesley, *Explanatory Notes on the NT*

"An indwelling Christ and GLORY; no indwelling Christ, NO glory." –Adam Clarke, A Commentary and Critical Notes.

"The Son of God who died and rose again is the embodiment of "the eternal life which was with the Father and was made manifest to us," so that to have "the Son" is to have "the life" and failure to have Him means forfeiture of "the life." –F. F. Bruce, *The Gospel & Epistles of John*

The Bottom line: Either you have life or you don't. Does the Son remain in a life that has departed its first love?

> **Notes:**

Revelation 3:5 (NIV)
[5] He who overcomes will, like them, be dressed in white. I will never blot out his name from the book of life, but will acknowledge his name before my Father and his angels.

Context: Christ's Message to the Three Churches

Calvinist View:

"This is a warning to live for God because no one knows what hour or date Jesus Christ may return. This is not a warning that your name will be blotted out of the book of Life, or that you can lose your salvation." –Elmer Towns, *Bible Answers for Almost All Your Questions*

Arminian Response: God would not have used a fake worst–case scenario argument. This is not metaphorical. It is using a possible warning to show His love and security offered to Believers.

Comment: This is not an empty argument, but plain fact. He who overcomes shows faith lived out. Otherwise the faith would be false and not genuine, and not of savable quality. This is not a general Book of living creatures as some have said, but the Book of life.

Quick Points:

1) This is not an empty or metaphorical argument.

2) This is looking at the positive side (will never blot out name) of a potentially critical situation (name blotted out).

3) The assurance is for the overcoming saint.

From the Experts:

"**And I will not blot his name out of the book of life** – Like that of the angel of the church at Sardis: but he shall live for ever.

I will confess his name – As one of my faithful servants and soldiers. – John Wesley, *Explanatory Notes upon the New Testament.*

The Bottom line: Overcoming sin and Satan leads to security.

Notes:

Revelation 5:9 (NIV)

[9] And they sang a new song: "You are worthy to take the scroll and to open its seals, because you were slain, and with your blood you purchased men for God from every tribe and language and people and nation.

Context: Scene: Heaven

Calvinist View: This would be the elect found in every people group across the Earth.

Arminian Response: John shows the wide scope of Christ's salvation that spans the globe.

Comment: John mentions that Jesus had "purchased men for God from every tribe and language and people and nation," through His Blood. These are not the pre-planned elect, but souls obedient to grace that fill out the elect category, known to God.

Quick Points:

1) Jesus' salvation crosses borders and people groups.

2) It is inclusive through grace, not exclusive to a decree.

From the Experts:

"Christ has redeemed his people from the bondage of sin, guilt, and Satan. He has not only purchased liberty for them, but the highest honour and preferment; he made them kings and priests; kings, to rule over their own spirits, and to overcome the world, and the evil one; and he makes them priests; giving them access to himself, and liberty to offer up spiritual sacrifices." –Matthew Henry, *Matthew Henry Concise Bible Commentary.*

The Bottom line: Jesus has pruchased salvation through His Blood for sinners, with the condition of belief.

Notes:

Passages you find that this study missed...
Text:

Context:

Calvinist View:

Arminian Response:

Comment:

Quick Points:

From the Experts:

The Bottom line:

Notes:

Text:

Context:

Calvinist View:

Arminian Response:

Comment:

Quick Points:

From the Experts:

The Bottom line:

Notes:

Text:

Context:

Calvinist View:

Arminian Response:

Comment:

Quick Points:

From the Experts:

The Bottom line:

Notes:

"Even I can have a new heart?"

Wesley's 30 Texts[1] *(notes added by author)*

Passage	Significance
Ezekiel 36:25, 26, 29	A new heart is promised for sinful people.
Matthew 5:8	The pure in heart see God.
Matthew 5:48	Christian perfection (completion of experience), not absolute.

[1] Holy Bible, *The Wesley Bible*. Thomas Nelson Publishers: Nashville, TN, 1990.

Matthew 6:10	The desire for the Father's will to be done is the right setting of the believer.
Matthew 22:37	Jesus quoted Deuteronomy 6:5, to drive home God's desire to be loved by His followers in wholeness of heart, soul, and mind, and to live out this love to other humans.
John 8:34-36	The Son can make the believer free from the power and pull of sin.
John 17:17, 20-23	God's truth sanctifies the Christian. It is God's will for oneness through the Spirit to be achieved perfectly (completely).
Romans 2:29	Circumcision of the heart is not to be a fantasy, but reality.
Romans 12:1, 2	Living sacrificially before God is what our purpose is, and avoiding defilement by the world.
2 Corinthians 7:1	Being cleansed from spiritual filthiness and being completed in holiness is activating God's promises.
Galatians 2:20	Losing selfish determination and finding Christ-likeness is living out Jesus' crucifixion.
Ephesians 3:14-19	Being strengthened in the "inner man" and filled with the fullness of God, is full Christian experience in this life.
Ephesians 5:27	To be holy, without spot or wrinkle, is God's plan for His church on Earth– while on Earth, accomplished through perfection of spiritual experience in Christ.
Philippians 3:15	Christian maturity is God's calling on humanity fulfilled.
1 Thessalonians 5:23	God's sanctification is to be a whole experience on Earth for the believer: in spirit, soul and body.
Titus 2:11-14	God's grace given through salvation makes it possible to resist fleshly living, and live a godly life "in this present age."
Hebrews 6:1	The elementary principles of Christ are to be steps to the deeper principles, resulting in a perfect Christian experience.
Hebrews 7:25	God's salvation is capable of saving "to the uttermost."
Hebrews 10:14	Those being sanctified (starting on Earth) are rooted in Christ's perfect sacrifice.
Hebrews 12:14	Holiness is not a way, but the way to see the Lord.
James 1:4	God's Spirit can work perfectly in us and yield us the experience of lacking nothing spiritually.

1 John 1:5, 7	Our walk must match our talk or we are deceived. Fellowship is in Christ's light, where cleansing from all the effects of sin is complete (sins/ nature).
1 John 1:8, 9	We cannot successfully deny our sin, so we need to have our sins forgiven by Christ and be cleansed from all unrighteousness.
1 John 3:3	The hope of being a child of God, brings with it a purifying experience, pure as He is pure.
1 John 3:8-10	Sinning is not God's plan. In fact those who sin as practice and habit is not a practitioner of righteousness (regardless of spiritual position) and in line with the Devil.
1 John 5:13	We need to know (begin the experience) that we are saved, and continue to believe in Christ. This is saved by grace, but proven by works.

Suggestions for Further Study

In the pages that follow, we have included some suggestions for further study that arose out of the research for this project:

Lesson 1 – Total Depravity

Lesson 2 – The Sovereignty of God

Lesson 3 – For *Whosoever* Believes

Lesson 4 – For Whosoever *Believes*

Lesson 5 – Blessed Assurance

James Lovaas

P246 Marketing Group

Lesson 1 - Depravity & Sin

Sin has typically been defined in one of two ways. First, there is the concept of missing the mark. Any act that falls short of God's will could be defined as sin. A second definition that John Wesley is credited with is "the willful trangression of the known law of God." Virtually all discussions regarding sin can fall somewhere between the two definitions. But...what is depravity? Dictionaries have defined it as a moral corruption. A wicked or morally corrupt act. The opening pages of this work listed total depravity under both Calvinism and Arminianism:

> **Arminianism -** Fallen spiritual nature from Adam (Original Sin). God provides grace to enable spiritual restoration through sanctification.

> **Calvinism -** Due to Adam's fall humans are irreparably fallen and must sin in thought, word, and deed. God has already saved the human, before they believe.

Consider the following passages:

Ephesians 2:1-10
Romans 3:9-20
Romans 8:7-8

For further discussion:

1. Can the believer experience freedom from depravity? If so, how much freedom?
2. Is the freedom permanent or is it contingent on one's relationship with God?
3. A 4th century monk named Pelagius, said that humans were not affected by the sinning and Fall of humanity in the Garden of Eden. How is this different from the Arminian view of depravity?

James Arminius wrote *"St. Augustine, after having diligently meditated upon each word in this passage, speaks thus: 'Christ does not say, without me you can do but little; neither does He say, without me you can do any difficult thing, nor without me you can do it with difficulty. But he says, without me you can do nothing!'"*

Lesson 2 – The Sovereignty of God

There is a natural struggle for the believer to accept both the concept of freewill, as well as the reality of the sovereignty of God. There have been those throughout the ages that have written that Wesleyan-Arminian theology actually denies the soverignty of God. But, what does it mean to say God is sovereign? Roger Olson has outlined two primary views of sovereignty that he calls divine determinism, and relational theism. The first position indicates that everything is caused by God and can be traced back to Him. Relational theism, however, indicates that there is real interactivity between God and man. Mildred Wynkoop has written that God's sovereignty allows man genuine freedom, but that freedom has its limits.

Throughout this work, the reader has been challenged to consider the scriptures in light of Arminian theology. None of these is in contradiction, or even limits, the sovereignty of God. In light of the earlier work, please consider the following scriptures:

Colossians 1:16-18
Jeremiah 32:17
Psalm 103:19
Revelation 21:6-8

In his work, The Knowledge of the Holy, A.W. Tozer wrote:

> *God sovereignly decreed that man should be free to exercise moral choice, and man from the beginning has fulfilled that decree by making his choice between good and evil. When he chooses to do evil, he does not thereby countervail the sovereign will of God but fulfills it, inasmuch as the eternal decree decided not which choice the man should make but that he should be free to make it. If in His absolute freedom God has willed to give man limited freedom, who is there to stay His hand or say, "What doest thou?" Man's will is free because God is sovereign. A God less than sovereign could not bestow moral freedom upon His creatures. He would be afraid to do so.*

For further discussion:

1. How does our freewill fit with the concept of a sovereign God?
2. How does God's sovereignty and impartial love fit together?

Lesson 3 - For *Whosoever* Believes

For God so loved the world, that he gave his only begotten Son, that whosoever believeth in him should not perish, but have everlasting life.
John 3:16 (KJV)

The third point of the Calvinist acronym TULIP stands for limited atonement – Jesus died only for the elect. Yet, the most natural reading of the most oft repeated verse in Christendom is the exact opposite. God, in His love, sent Jesus for whosoever…for all who believe.

In John chapter three, Jesus tells Nicodemus that "no one can see the kingdom of God unless they are born again." Jesus challenges Nicodemus. He says that Nicodemus is one of Israel's teachers, yet he doesn't understand these simple truths. Jesus then says, "just as Moses lifted up the snake in the wilderness, so the Son of Man must be lifted up, that *everyone who believes may have eternal life in him.*"

Yet, John 3:15-16 are far from the only verses to reflect this understanding. Consider the following passages:

> John 3:18
> John 3:31-36
> John 5:24
> 1 John 5:1
> 1 John 5:10

For further discussion:

1. What will you do with Romans 8:29-30? How does it fit with the passages above?
2. How do the above passages affect you emotionally?
3. How should the promise that salvation is available to all impact your daily life?

"But Jesus did not preach to the multitudes as though they were a faceless crowd. He preached to them as individuals…Each of us must come with full confidence that it is a personal word God has spoken to us in Christ, that whosoever believeth in Him shall not perish."
A.W. Tozer

Lesson 4 - For Whosoever *Believes*

For God so loved the world, that he gave his only begotten Son, that whosoever believeth in him should not perish, but have everlasting life.
John 3:16 (KJV)

According to a 2012 GallupPoll, 75% of Americans identify themselves as members of a Christian religion. That is to say, they claim some form of membership in one of any number of Catholic or protestant denominations. However, almost 75% of those respondents claim to rarely, if ever, attend a worship service. So, what does it really mean to "believe" in Jesus?

Read Romans chapter 10 and pay special attention to:
>Romans 10:9-10
>Romans 10:14

But, what does it mean to believe in one's heart? Consider the words of James, the brother of Jesus:

What good is it, my brothers and sisters, if someone claims to have faith but has no deeds? Can such faith save them? Suppose a brother or a sister is without clothes and daily food. If one of you says to them, "Go in peace; keep warm and well fed," but does nothing about their physical needs, what good is it? In the same way, faith by itself, if it is not accompanied by action, is dead. (James 2:14-17, NIV)

In the New Testament there is no contradiction between faith and obedience. Between faith and law-works, yes; between law and grace, yes; but between faith and obedience, not at all. The Bible recognizes no faith that does not lead to obedience, nor does it recognize any obedience that does not spring from faith. (A.W. Tozer – Paths to Power)

For further discussion:
1. How do we explain or describe a belief that goes beyond simple intellectual certainty?
2. How do we explain Paul's words: "it is with your mouth that you profess your faith and are saved"?
3. While true faith and belief leads to outward works, how do we avoid a works based faith?

Doug West

Lesson 5 - Blessed Assurance

The Spirit himself testifies with our spirit that we are God's children. 17 Now if we are children, then we are heirs—heirs of God and co-heirs with Christ, if indeed we share in his sufferings in order that we may also share in his glory.
Romans 8:16-17 (NIV)

There have been, and will continue to be, discussions surrounding the Wesleyan view of conditional preservation - described here as the believer being secure as they actively remain "in Christ." God's grace never stops calling the sinner on the run, but freewill allows for a departure from grace. Yet, we ought never forget that *the Spirit himself testifies with our spirit that we are God's children...*

Consider the following passages:
> Romans 8:1-17
> John 5:24-27
> John 15:1-7

Many a believer has struggled under a theology that has led to the belief that salvation is lost and found throughout one's life. Yet the Scriptures do not paint such a picture. After reading the passages above, take a few moments to consider your own sense of assurance.

For further discussion:
1. What does it mean to "remain in Him"?
2. What does it mean when Paul writes that "the Spirit himself testifies with our spirit that we are God's children"?
3. How do we reconcile the doctrine of conditional preservation and the fact that we can sure of our salvation?
4. Why does it even matter?

No condemnation now I dread;
Jesus, and all in Him, is mine;
Alive in Him, my living Head,
And clothed in righteousness divine,
Bold I approach th'eternal throne,
And claim the crown, through Christ my own.
(And Can it Be - Charles Wesley)

Glossary of Terms

Arminianism- The theology of James Arminius that challenged the Calvinist community by stating that salvation was conditional, and souls were free to choose God as opposed to being predestined. His followers came up with Five Points in a Remonstrance (protest) opposing Calvinism.

Called- God has invited humans to be called to salvation.

Calvinism- the theology of John Calvin that stressed strong Sovereignty and Predestination of souls.

Canon of Scripture- "standard," the ordering and attributing of Divine inspiration to the 66 books of the Bible by a church council.

Election- God chose the Israelite nation above all other nations, and chooses some believers for distinct service (The Prophet Jeremiah, The Apostle Paul), and sets salvation to be received by all who are willing.

Entire sanctification- A second work of God's grace that occurs in a moment time, subsequent to salvation, when the Holy Spirit takes out the sin nature.

Foreknowledge- God knows things beforehand like who will be saved.

Freewill- Sometimes called freedom of the will or free agency/ free moral agency. It is a tool God has given humans to choose or reject Him at any part of the journey. It is not mere human determination of will (apart from God).

Glorification- The nature of salvation in heaven where all flaws are removed and the human is perfected.

Grace- Unmerited favor show by God to the just and the unjust.

Initial sanctification- a theological term that is sometimes given to salvation.

Omniscience- God is all knowing.

Omnipotence- God is all-powerful.

Omnipresence- God is everywhere at once, and yet can be personal as well. He is not everything, but everywhere.

Predestination- God planned before time that humanity should receive the plan of salvation. Those who receive Jesus have made good on their calling and election and are called saints.

Prevenient Grace- God's grace that reaches out to souls, before, during, and after salvation and entire sanctification. (Romans 5:8)

Salvation History- The building and revealing of God's Plan for Jesus the Messiah to come, in which people and places laid a foundation for His line (David) to be established.

Sovereign- God is in total control of all and everything.

Wesleyan- The theology of John Wesley that promoted free grace and entire sanctification of believers.

God's Plan of Salvation for You…

A- Admit you are a sinner. (Romans 3:23)

B- Believe that Jesus can fix your sin problem. (Romans 6:23)

C- Confess Jesus as Lord. (Romans 10:9, 10)

Contact us for further help or support with this. salvation@p246.net
Other helpful Links:
billygraham.org
focusonthefamily.com

Bibliography
Books

Applebee, Dennis. *When I Tread The Verge of the Jordan.* World Gospel Mission: Marion, IN, 1988.

Arminius, J., Complete Works of Arminius. Public Domain. 2010.

Arthur, Kay. *Lord, I Need Grace To Make It.* Multnomah Press: Portland, OR, 1989.

Board of General Superintendents, Church of the Nazarene. *Blameless At His Coming and Other Sermons.* Beacon Hill Press: Kansas City, MO, 2009.

Bruce, F.F. *The Gospel & Epistles of John.* William B. Eerdman's Publishing Company: Grand Rapids, MI, 1983.

Coppedge, Allan. *The Biblical Principles of Discipleship.* Francis Asbury Press/Zondervan: Grand Rapids, MI, 1989.

Eby, J. Wesley, Lyons, George & Truesdale, Al. *A Dictionary of the Bible & Christian Doctrine in Everyday English.* Beacon Hill Press: 2004.

Elwell, Walter A. *Evangelical Dictionary of Theology, Second Ed.* Baker Book House: Grand Rapids, MI, 2001.

Erickson, Millard J. *Christian Theology.* Baker Books: Grand Rapids, MI, 1998.

Greathouse, William M. and Ray Dunning. *An Introduction to Wesleyan Theology.* Beacon Hill Press: Kansas City, MO, 1982.

Holy Bible, *The Wesley Bible.* Thomas Nelson Publishers: Nashville, TN, 1990.

Jessop, Harry E. *Foundations of Doctrine.* Vennard College: University Park, IA, 1938.

Jones, E. Stanley. *Conversion.* Abingdon Press: Nashville, TN, 1959.

Lewis, C. S. *Mere Christianity.* Macmillan Publishing Co: New York, NY, 1960.

Lovett, Danny. Jesus is Awesome. 21st Century Press: Springfield, MO, 2003.

Lutzer, Irwin W. *How in This World Can I Be Holy?* Moody Press: Chicago, IL, 1985.

MacArthur, John. Saved Without a Doubt. Victor books: Wheaton, Ill, 1992.

MacArthur, John. The MacArthur Study Bible. Thomas Nelson: Nashville, TN, 1997.

Marshall, I. Howard. *Kept By the Power of God.* Wipf and Stock Publishers: Eugene, OR, 1969.

McGee, J. Vernon. *Who Is God?* Thomas Nelson Publishers: Nashville, TN, 1999.

Moore, Frank. *Coffee Shop Theology*: Beacon Hill Press: Kansas City, MO, 1998.

Morgan, G. Campbell. *An Exposition of the Whole Bible.* Fleming H. Revell: Grand Rapids, MI, 1959.

Moore, Frank. *More Coffee Shop Theology*: Beacon Hill Press: Kansas City, MO, 1998.

Metz, Donald S. *Studies in Biblical Holiness.* Beacon Hill Press: Kansas City, MO, 1971.

Nee, Watchman. *Love not the World.* Christian Literature Crusade: Port Washington, PA, 1972.

Nee, Watchman. *The Normal Christian Life.* CLC/ Tyndale House Publishers: Wheaton, IL, 1978.

Oswalt, John N. *Called to be Holy.* Evangel Publ. House: Nappanee, IN, 1999.

Purkiser, W.T. ed. *Exploring Our Christian Faith.* Beacon Hill Press: Kansas City, MO, 1978.

Purkiser, W.T. *Security, The False & the True.* Beacon Hill Press: Kansas City, MO, 1974.

Purkiser, W.T., Richard S. Taylor, Willard H. Taylor. *God, Man, and Salvation.* Beacon Hill Press: Kansas City, MO, 1977.

Richard, Dr, Ramesh P. *The Population of Heaven.*   Moody Press: Chicago, IL, 1994.

Roberts, B.T. *Holiness Teachings.* H.E. Schmul, 1893.

Shank, Robert, *Elect in the Son.* Wescott Publ: Springfield, MO, 1970.

Shank, Robert. *Life in the Son.* Bethany House Publishing: Minneapolis, MN, 1989.

Snyder, Howard A. *The Radical Wesley.* InterVarsity Press: Downers Grove, IL, 1980.

Swindoll, Charles. *Growing Deeper in the Christian Life.* Multnomah Press: Portland, OR, 1986.

Taylor, Richard S. *A Right Conception of Sin.* Beacon Hill Press: Kansas City, MO, 1945.

Taylor, Richard S., J. Kenneth Grider, Willard H. Taylor, ed. *Beacon Dictionary of Theology.* Beacon Hill Press: Kansas City, MO, 1983.

Taylor, Richard Shelley. *The Disciplined Life.* Beacon Hill Press: Kansas City, MO, 1962.

Towns, Elmer. *Bible Answers For Almost All Your Questions.* Thomas Nelson Publishers: Nashville, TN, 2003.

Tozer, A.W. *Of God and Men.* Christian Publ, Inc: Harrisburg, PN, 1960.

Tozer, A.W. Paths to Power. Crane Books: Chalfont, PA, 2013.

Tozer, A.W. *The Pursuit of God.* Christian Publ. Inc: Camp Hill, PN, 1982.

Tozer, A.W. *The Knowledge of the Holy.* Harper Collins: San Francisco, CA, 1961.

Vos, Howard F. *Exploring Church History.* Thomas Nelson Publishers: Nashville, TN, 1994.

Unger, Merrill F. *Unger's Commentary on the Whole Bible.*

Wilkerson, David. Victory over Sin and Self. Fleming H. Revell: Grand Rapids, MI,

Wynkoop, Mildred Bangs. *Foundations of Wesleyan-Arminian Theology.* Beacon Hill Press: 1967.

Electronic Books

Barnes, Albert. Barnes Notes on the Whole Bible.
http://www.studylight.org

Calvin, John. Commentaries on the Bible. http://www.studylight.org

The Geneva Study Bible. http://www.studylight.org

Girardeau, John L. *Calvinism and Evangelical Arminianism: Compared as to Election, Reprobation, Justification, and Related Doctrines.* The Baker & Taylor Co: New York, NY, 1890, NOOK.

Hunter, A. Mitchell. *The Teaching of Calvin, A Modern Interpretation.* Maclehose, Jackson and Co: Glasgow, 1920, NOOK.

Hodge, Charles. *Arminianism and Grace.* James Bain and Sons: Toronto, 1881, NOOK.

Hunt, Dave and James White. *Debating Calvinism.* Multnomah Books, NOOK.

Long, H.A. *Calvinism Popularised.* James Nisbet & Co: London, 1895, NOOK.

Olson, R. E.. *Arminian Theology: Myths and Realities.* IVP Academic: Downers Grove, IL, 2006, Kindle Edition.

Philalethes. *A Solemn Caution Against the Ten Horns of Calvinism.* James Nichols, 1819, NOOK.

Strong, J. Selden. *The Essential Calvinism.* The Pilgrim Press: Boston, MA, 1909, NOOK.

Electronic Journals

Bryant, Barry E. Molina, Arminius, Plaifere, Goad, and Wesley on Human Free-Will, Divine Omniscience, and Middle Knowledge. *Wesleyan Theological Journal* Vol. 27, 1992: 93-103.
http://wesley.nnu.edu/fileadmin/imported_site/wesleyjournal/1992-wtj-27.pdf

Callen, Barry L. From Tulip to Rose: Clark H. Pinnock on the Open and Risking God." *Wesleyan Theological Journal* Vol. 1, Vol. 36, Spring 2001: 160-186.
http://wesley.nnu.edu/fileadmin/imported_site/wesleyjournal/2001-wtj-36-1.pdf

Cox, Leo G. "Sin in Believers." *Wesleyan Theological Journal* Vol. 1, Spring 1966: 27-31.
http://wesley.nnu.edu/fileadmin/imported_site/wesleyjournal/1966-wtj-01.pdf

Gunter, W. Stephen. "John Wesley, Explanatory Notes on the NT, A Faithful Representative of Jacob Arminius." *Wesleyan Theological Journal* Vol. 42, Number 2, Fall 2007: 65-80.
http://wesley.nnu.edu/fileadmin/imported_site/wesleyjournal/2007-wtj-02.pdf

Kinghorn, Kenneth. "Biblical Concepts of Sin." *Wesleyan Theological Journal* Vol. 1, Spring 1966: 21-26.
http://wesley.nnu.edu/fileadmin/imported_site/wesleyjournal/1966-wtj-01.pdf

Maddox, Randy. "Responsible Grace: The Systematic Perspective of Wesleyan Theology." *Wesleyan Theological Journal* Vol. 19, Number 2, Fall 1984: 7-22.
http://wesley.nnu.edu/fileadmin/imported_site/wesleyjournal/1966-wtj-01.pdf

Newport, Frank. "In U.S., 77% Identify as Christian." Gallup Politics
http://www.gallup.com/poll/159548/identify-christian.aspx

Taylor, Richard S. "The Question of "Sins of Ignorance" in Relation to Wesley's Definition." *Wesleyan Theological Journal* Vol. 22, Number 1, Spring 1987: 84-91.
http://wesley.nnu.edu/fileadmin/imported_site/wesleyjournal/1987-wtj-22-2.pdf

Software

WORDSearch 9, CBD Pastor's Addition, *Warren Wiersbe, The Bible Exposition Commentary (Be Series), New Testament, Volume 1,* E-Book, Austin, TX: WORDSearchBible, 2004.

WORDSearch 9, CBD Pastor's Addition, *A. W. Tozer, I Talk Back to the Devil: Straightforward Appeals for Christlike Living.*, E-Book, Austin, TX: WORDSearchBible, 2004.

WORDSearch 9, CBD Pastor's Addition, *John Calvin, Institutes of the Christian Religion.* Trans. by Henry Beveridge, Esq. Institutes of the Christian Religion., CD-ROM, TX: WORDSearchBible, 2007.

WORDSearch 9, CBD Pastor's Addition, *The Complete Works of James Arminius, Vol. 1-3.* Trans. by James Nichols, and William R. Bagnall, CD-ROM, Austin, TX: WORDSearchBible, 2004.

www.ingramcontent.com/pod-product-compliance
Lightning Source LLC
Chambersburg PA
CBHW071958040426
42447CB00009B/1382